COLLECTED POEMS

COLLECTED POEMS

COLLECTED POEMS

by

SIEGFRIED SASSOON

FABER AND FABER LIMITED
24 Russell Square
London

First published in Mcmxlvii
by Faber and Faber Limited
24 Russell Square London W.C. 1
Printed in Great Britain by
R. MacLehose and Company Limited
The University Press Glasgow

Microcosmos

I am that fantasy which race has wrought
Of mundane chance-material. I am time
Paeaned by the senses five like bells that chime.

I am that cramped and crumbling house of clay
Where mansoul weaves the secret webs of thought.
Venturer—automaton—I cannot tell
What powers and instincts animate and betray
And do their dreamwork in me. Seed and star,
Sown by the wind, in spirit I am far
From self, the dull control with whom I dwell.

Also I am ancestral. Aeons ahead
And ages back, both son and sire I live
Mote-like between the unquickened and the dead—
From whom I take, and unto whom I give.

[v]

Contents

[vii]

[viii]

COUNTER-ATTACK AND OTHER POEMS

[ix]

PICTURE-SHOW

[x]

SATIRICAL POEMS

[xii]

THE HEART'S JOURNEY

RHYMED RUMINATIONS

[xvi]

THE OLD HUNTSMAN
AND
OTHER POEMS

A   S.C.P.

I

The Old Huntsman

I've never ceased to curse the day I signed
A seven years' bargain for the Golden Fleece.
'Twas a bad deal all round; and dear enough
It cost me, what with my daft management,
And the mean folk as owed and never paid me,
And backing losers; and the local bucks
Egging me on with whiskys while I bragged
The man I was when huntsman to the Squire.

I'd have been prosperous if I'd took a farm
Of fifty acres, drove my gig and haggled
At Monday markets; now I've squandered all
My savings; nigh three hundred pound I got
As testimonial when I'd grown too stiff
And slow to press a beaten fox.

                   The Fleece!
'Twas the damned Fleece that wore my Emily out,
The wife of thirty years who served me well;
(Not like this beldam clattering in the kitchen,
That never trims a lamp nor sweeps the floor,
And brings me greasy soup in a foul crock.)

Blast the old harridan! What's fetched her now,
Leaving me in the dark, and short of fire?

[3]

And where's my pipe? 'Tis lucky I've a turn
For thinking, and remembering all that's past.
And now's my hour, before I hobble to bed,
To set the works a-wheezing, wind the clock
That keeps the time of life with feeble tick
Behind my bleared old face that stares and wonders.

It's queer how, in the dark, comes back to mind
Some morning of September. We've been digging
In a steep sandy warren, riddled with holes,
And I've just pulled the terrier out and left
A sharp-nosed cub-face blinking there and snapping,
Then in a moment seen him mobbed and torn
To strips in the baying hurly of the pack.
I picture it so clear : the dusty sunshine
On bracken, and the men with spades, that wipe
Red faces : one tilts up a mug of ale.
And, having stopped to clean my gory hands,
I whistle the jostling beauties out of the wood.

I'm but a daft old fool! I often wish
The Squire were back again—ah! he was a man!
They don't breed men like him these days ; he'd come
For sure, and sit and talk and suck his briar
Till the old wife brings up a dish of tea.

Ay, those were days, when I was serving Squire!
I never knowed such sport as '85,
The winter afore the one that snowed us silly.

Once in a way the parson will drop in
And read a bit o' the Bible, if I'm bad,
And pray the Lord to make my spirit whole
In faith : he leaves some 'baccy on the shelf,
And wonders I don't keep a dog to cheer me
Because he knows I'm mortal fond of dogs!

I ask you, what's a gent like that to me
As wouldn't know Elijah if I saw him,
Nor have the wit to keep him on the talk?
'Tis kind of parson to be troubling still
With such as me; but he's a town-bred chap,
Full of his college notions and Christmas hymns.

Religion beats me. I'm amazed at folk
Drinking the gospels in and never scratching
Their heads for questions. When I was a lad
I learned a bit from mother, and never thought
To educate myself for prayers and psalms.

But now I'm old and bald and serious-minded,
With days to sit and ponder. I'd no chance
When young and gay to get the hang of all
This Hell and Heaven : and when the clergy hoick
And holloa from their pulpits, I'm asleep,
However hard I listen; and when they pray
It seems we're all like children sucking sweets
In school, and wondering whether master sees.

I used to dream of Hell when I was first
Promoted to a huntsman's job, and scent
Was rotten, and all the foxes disappeared,

[5]

And hounds were short of blood; and officers
From barracks over-rode 'em all day long
On weedy, whistling nags that knocked a hole
In every fence; good sportsmen to a man
And brigadiers by now, but dreadful hard
On a young huntsman keen to show some sport.

Ay, Hell was thick with captains, and I rode
The lumbering brute that's beat in half a mile,
And blunders into every blind old ditch.
Hell was the coldest scenting land I've known,
And both my whips were always lost, and hounds
Would never get their heads down; and a man
On a great yawing chestnut trying to cast 'em
While I was in a corner pounded by
The ugliest hog-backed stile you've clapped your eyes on.
There was an iron-spiked fence round all the coverts,
And civil-spoken keepers I couldn't trust,
And the main earth unstopp'd. The fox I found
Was always a three-legged 'un from a bag,
Who reeked of aniseed and wouldn't run.
The farmers were all ploughing their old pasture
And bellowing at me when I rode their beans
To cast for beaten fox, or galloped on
With hounds to a lucky view. I'd lost my voice
Although I shouted fit to burst my guts,
And couldn't blow my horn.

                              And when I woke,
Emily snored, and barn-cocks started crowing,
And morn was at the window; and I was glad
To be alive because I heard the cry

Of hounds like church-bells chiming on a Sunday.
Ay, that's the song I'd wish to hear in Heaven!
The cry of hounds was Heaven for me : I know
Parson would call me crazed and wrong to say it,
But where's the use of life and being glad
If God's not in your gladness ?

                            I've no brains
For book-learned studies ; but I've heard men say
There's much in print that clergy have to wink at :
Though many I've met were jolly chaps, and rode
To hounds, and walked me puppies ; and could pick
Good legs and loins and necks and shoulders, ay,
And feet—'twas necks and feet I looked at first.

Some hounds I've known were wise as half your saints,
And better hunters. That old dog of the Duke's,
Harlequin ; what a dog he was to draw!
And what a note he had, and what a nose
When foxes ran down wind and scent was catchy!
And that light lemon bitch of the Squire's, old Dorcas—
She were a marvellous hunter, were old Dorcas!
Ay, oft I've thought, 'If there were hounds in Heaven,
With God as master, taking no subscription ;
And all His blessèd country farmed by tenants,
And a straight-necked old fox in every gorse!'
But when I came to work it out, I found
There'd be too many huntsmen wanting places,
Though some I've known might get a job with Nick!

I've come to think of God as something like
The figure of a man the old Duke was
When I was turning hounds to Nimrod King,
Before his Grace was took so bad with gout
And had to quit the saddle. Tall and spare,
Clean-shaved and grey, with shrewd, kind eyes, that
    twinkled,
And easy walk; who, when he gave good words,
Gave them whole-hearted; and would never blame
Without just cause. Lord God might be like that,
Sitting alone in a great room of books
Some evening after hunting.

                      Now I'm tired
With hearkening to the tick-tack on the shelf;
And pondering makes me doubtful.

                      Riding home
On a moonless night of cloud that feels like frost
Though stars are hidden (hold your feet up, horse!)
And thinking what a task I had to draw
A pack with all those lame 'uns, and the lot
Wanting a rest from all this open weather;
That's what I'm doing now.

                      And likely, too,
The frost'll be a long 'un, and the night
One sleep. The parsons say we'll wake to find
A country blinding-white with dazzle of snow.

The naked stars make men feel lonely, wheeling
And glinting on the puddles in the road.

And then you listen to the wind, and wonder
If folk are quite such bucks as they appear
When dressed by London tailors, looking down
Their boots at covert side, and thinking big.

This world's a funny place to live in. Soon
I'll need to change my country; but I know
'Tis little enough I've understood my life,
And a power of sights I've missed, and foreign marvels.

I used to feel it, riding on spring days
In meadows pied with sun and chasing clouds,
And half forget how I was there to catch
The foxes; lose the angry, eager feeling
A huntsman ought to have, that's out for blood,
And means his hounds to get it!

                                        Now I know
It's God that speaks to us when we're bewitched,
Smelling the hay in June and smiling quiet;
Or when there's been a spell of summer drought,
Lying awake and listening to the rain.

I'd like to be the simpleton I was
In the old days when I was whipping-in
To a little harrier-pack in Worcestershire,
And loved a dairymaid, but never knew it
Until she'd wed another. So I've loved
My life; and when the good years are gone down,
Discover what I've lost.

[9]

                                I never broke
Out of my blundering self into the world,
But let it all go past me, like a man
Half asleep in a land that's full of wars.

What a grand thing 'twould be if I could go
Back to the kennels now and take my hounds
For summer exercise; be riding out
With forty couple when the quiet skies
Are streaked with sunrise, and the silly birds
Grown hoarse with singing; cobwebs on the furze
Up on the hill, and all the country strange,
With no one stirring; and the horses fresh,
Sniffing the air I'll never breathe again.

                 .   .   .   .

You've brought the lamp, then, Martha? I've no mind
For newspaper to-night, nor bread and cheese.
Give me the candle, and I'll get to bed.

II
WAR POEMS: 1915-1917

Absolution

The anguish of the earth absolves our eyes
Till beauty shines in all that we can see.
War is our scourge; yet war has made us wise,
And, fighting for our freedom, we are free.

Horror of wounds and anger at the foe,
And loss of things desired; all these must pass.
We are the happy legion, for we know
Time's but a golden wind that shakes the grass.

There was an hour when we were loth to part
From life we longed to share no less than others.
Now, having claimed this heritage of heart,
What need we more, my comrades and my brothers?

To My Brother

Give me your hand, my brother, search my face;
Look in these eyes lest I should think of shame;
For we have made an end of all things base.
We are returning by the road we came.

Your lot is with the ghosts of soldiers dead,
And I am in the field where men must fight.
But in the gloom I see your laurell'd head
And through your victory I shall win the light.

The Dragon and the Undying

All night the flares go up; the Dragon sings
And beats upon the dark with furious wings;
And, stung to rage by his own darting fires,
Reaches with grappling coils from town to town;
He lusts to break the loveliness of spires,
And hurls their martyred music toppling down.

Yet, though the slain are homeless as the breeze,
Vocal are they, like storm-bewilder'd seas.
Their faces are the fair, unshrouded night,
And planets are their eyes, their ageless dreams.
Tenderly stooping earthward from their height,
They wander in the dusk with chanting streams,
And they are dawn-lit trees, with arms up-flung,
To hail the burning heavens they left unsung.

France

She triumphs, in the vivid green
Where sun and quivering foliage meet;
And in each soldier's heart serene;

When death stood near them they have seen
The radiant forests where her feet
Move on a breeze of silver sheen.

And they are fortunate, who fight
For gleaming landscapes swept and shafted
And crowned by cloud pavilions white;
Hearing such harmonies as might
Only from Heaven be downward wafted—
Voices of victory and delight.

To Victory

Return to greet me, colours that were my joy,
Not in the woeful crimson of men slain,
But shining as a garden; come with the streaming
Banners of dawn and sundown after rain.

I want to fill my gaze with blue and silver,
Radiance through living roses, spires of green
Rising in young-limbed copse and lovely wood
Where the hueless wind passes and cries unseen.

I am not sad; only I long for lustre.
I am tired of the greys and browns and the leafless ash.
I would have hours that move like a glitter of dancers
Far from the angry guns that boom and flash.

Return, musical, gay with blossom and fleetness,
Days when my sight shall be clear and my heart rejoice;

Come from the sea with breadth of approaching
    brightness,
When the blithe wind laughs on the hills with uplifted
    voice.

When I'm among a Blaze of Lights

When I'm among a blaze of lights,
With tawdry music and cigars
And women dawdling through delights,
And officers in cocktail bars,
Sometimes I think of garden nights
And elm trees nodding at the stars.

I dream of a small firelit room
With yellow candles burning straight,
And glowing pictures in the gloom,
And kindly books that hold me late.
Of things like these I choose to think
When I can never be alone:
Then someone says 'Another drink?'
And turns my living heart to stone.

Golgotha

Through darkness curves a spume of falling flares
That flood the field with shallow, blanching light.
    The huddled sentry stares
    On gloom at war with white,

And white receding slow, submerged in gloom.
Guns into mimic thunder burst and boom,
    And mirthless laughter rakes the whistling night.
The sentry keeps his watch where no one stirs
But the brown rats, the nimble scavengers.

A Mystic as Soldier

I lived my days apart,
Dreaming fair songs for God;
By the glory in my heart
Covered and crowned and shod.

Now God is in the strife,
And I must seek Him there,
Where death outnumbers life,
And fury smites the air.

I walk the secret way
With anger in my brain.
O music through my clay,
When will you sound again?

The Kiss

To these I turn, in these I trust—
Brother Lead and Sister Steel.
To his blind power I make appeal,
I guard her beauty clean from rust.

He spins and burns and loves the air,
And splits a skull to win my praise;
But up the nobly marching days
She glitters naked, cold and fair.

Sweet Sister, grant your soldier this:
That in good fury he may feel
The body where he sets his heel
Quail from your downward darting kiss.

The Redeemer

Darkness: the rain sluiced down; the mire was deep;
It was past twelve on a mid-winter night,
When peaceful folk in beds lay snug asleep;
There, with much work to do before the light,
We lugged our clay-sucked boots as best we might
Along the trench; sometimes a bullet sang,
And droning shells burst with a hollow bang;
We were soaked, chilled and wretched, every one;
Darkness; the distant wink of a huge gun.

I turned in the black ditch, loathing the storm;
A rocket fizzed and burned with blanching flare,
And lit the face of what had been a form
Floundering in mirk. He stood before me there;
I say that He was Christ; stiff in the glare,
And leaning forward from His burdening task,
Both arms supporting it; His eyes on mine
Stared from the woeful head that seemed a mask
Of mortal pain in Hell's unholy shine.

No thorny crown, only a woollen cap
He wore—an English soldier, white and strong,
Who loved his time like any simple chap,
Good days of work and sport and homely song;
Now he has learned that nights are very long,
And dawn a watching of the windowed sky.
But to the end, unjudging, he'll endure
Horror and pain, not uncontent to die
That Lancaster on Lune may stand secure.

He faced me, reeling in his weariness,
Shouldering his load of planks, so hard to bear.
I say that He was Christ, who wrought to bless
All groping things with freedom bright as air,
And with His mercy washed and made them fair.
Then the flame sank, and all grew black as pitch,
While we began to struggle along the ditch;
And someone flung his burden in the muck,
Mumbling: 'O Christ Almighty, now I'm stuck!'

A Subaltern

He turned to me with his kind, sleepy gaze
And fresh face slowly brightening to the grin
That sets my memory back to summer days,
With twenty runs to make, and last man in.
He told me he'd been having a bloody time
In trenches, crouching for the crumps to burst,
While squeaking rats scampered across the slime
And the grey palsied weather did its worst.

But as he stamped and shivered in the rain,
My stale philosophies had served him well;
Dreaming about his girl had sent his brain
Blanker than ever—she'd no place in Hell. . . .
'Good God!' he laughed, and slowly filled his pipe,
Wondering 'why he always talked such tripe'.

In the Pink

So Davies wrote: 'This leaves me in the pink'.
Then scrawled his name: 'Your loving sweetheart,
        Willie'.
With crosses for a hug. He'd had a drink
Of rum and tea; and, though the barn was chilly,
For once his blood ran warm; he had pay to spend.
Winter was passing; soon the year would mend.

But he couldn't sleep that night; stiff in the dark
He groaned and thought of Sundays at the farm,
And how he'd go as cheerful as a lark
In his best suit, to wander arm in arm
With brown-eyed Gwen, and whisper in her ear
The simple, silly things she liked to hear.

And then he thought: to-morrow night we trudge
Up to the trenches, and my boots are rotten.
Five miles of stodgy clay and freezing sludge,
And everything but wretchedness forgotten.
To-night he's in the pink; but soon he'll die.
And still the war goes on—*he* don't know why.

A Working Party

Three hours ago he blundered up the trench,
Sliding and poising, groping with his boots;
Sometimes he tripped and lurched against the walls
With hands that pawed the sodden bags of chalk.
He couldn't see the man who walked in front;
Only he heard the drum and rattle of feet
Stepping along barred trench boards, often splashing
Wretchedly where the sludge was ankle-deep.

Voices would grunt 'Keep to your right—make way!'
When squeezing past some men from the front-line:
White faces peered, puffing a point of red;
Candles and braziers glinted through the chinks
And curtain-flaps of dug-outs; then the gloom
Swallowed his sense of sight; he stooped and swore
Because a sagging wire had caught his neck.

A flare went up; the shining whiteness spread
And flickered upward, showing nimble rats
And mounds of glimmering sand-bags, bleached with
    rain;
Then the slow silver moment died in dark.
The wind came posting by with chilly gusts
And buffeting at corners, piping thin.
And dreary through the crannies; rifle-shots
Would split and crack and sing along the night,
And shells came calmly through the drizzling air
To burst with hollow bang below the hill.

Three hours ago he stumbled up the trench;
Now he will never walk that road again:
He must be carried back, a jolting lump
Beyond all need of tenderness and care.

He was a young man with a meagre wife
And two small children in a Midland town;
He showed their photographs to all his mates,
And they considered him a decent chap
Who did his work and hadn't much to say,
And always laughed at other people's jokes
Because he hadn't any of his own.

That night when he was busy at his job
Of piling bags along the parapet,
He thought how slow time went, stamping his feet
And blowing on his fingers, pinched with cold.
He thought of getting back by half-past twelve,
And tot of rum to send him warm to sleep
In draughty dug-out frowsty with the fumes
Of coke, and full of snoring weary men.

He pushed another bag along the top,
Craning his body outward; then a flare
Gave one white glimpse of No Man's Land and wire;
And as he dropped his head the instant split
His startled life with lead, and all went out.

A Whispered Tale

I'd heard fool-heroes brag of where they'd been,
With stories of the glories that they'd seen.
But you, good simple soldier, seasoned well
In woods and posts and crater-lines of hell,
Who dodge remembered 'crumps' with wry grimace,
Endured experience in your queer, kind face,
Fatigues and vigils haunting nerve-strained eyes,
And both your brothers killed to make you wise;
You had no babbling phrases; what you said
Was like a message from the maimed and dead.
But memory brought the voice I knew, whose note
Was muted when they shot you in the throat;
And still you whisper of the war, and find
Sour jokes for all those horrors left behind.

'Blighters'

The House is crammed: tier beyond tier they grin
And cackle at the Show, while prancing ranks
Of harlots shrill the chorus, drunk with din;
'We're sure the Kaiser loves our dear old Tanks!'

I'd like to see a Tank come down the stalls,
Lurching to rag-time tunes, or 'Home, sweet Home',
And there'd be no more jokes in Music-halls
To mock the riddled corpses round Bapaume.

At Carnoy

Down in the hollow there's the whole Brigade
Camped in four groups: through twilight falling slow
I hear a sound of mouth-organs, ill-played,
And murmur of voices, gruff, confused, and low.
Crouched among thistle-tufts I've watched the glow
Of a blurred orange sunset flare and fade;
And I'm content. To-morrow we must go
To take some cursèd Wood . . . O world God made!

July 3rd, 1916.

To His Dead Body

When roaring gloom surged inward and you cried,
Groping for friendly hands, and clutched, and died,
Like racing smoke, swift from your lolling head
Phantoms of thought and memory thinned and fled.

Yet, though my dreams that throng the darkened stair
Can bring me no report of how you fare,
Safe quit of wars, I speed you on your way
Up lonely, glimmering fields to find new day,
Slow-rising, saintless, confident and kind—
Dear, red-faced father God who lit your mind.

Two Hundred Years After

Trudging by Corbie Ridge one winter's night,
(Unless old hearsay memories tricked his sight)
Along the pallid edge of the quiet sky
He watched a nosing lorry grinding on,
And straggling files of men; when these were gone,
A double limber and six mules went by,
Hauling the rations up through ruts and mud
To trench-lines digged two hundred years ago.
Then darkness hid them with a rainy scud,
And soon he saw the village lights below.

But when he'd told his tale, an old man said
That *he'd* seen soldiers pass along that hill;
'Poor silent things, they were the English dead
Who came to fight in France and got their fill.'

'They'

The Bishop tells us: 'When the boys come back
'They will not be the same; for they'll have fought
'In a just cause: they lead the last attack
'On Anti-Christ; their comrades' blood has bought
'New right to breed an honourable race,
'They have challenged Death and dared him face to face.'

'We're none of us the same!' the boys reply.
'For George lost both his legs; and Bill's stone blind;

[23]

'Poor Jim's shot through the lungs and like to die;
'And Bert's gone syphilitic: you'll not find
'A chap who's served that hasn't found *some* change.'
And the Bishop said: 'The ways of God are strange!'

Stand-to: Good Friday Morning

I'd been on duty from two till four.
I went and stared at the dug-out door.
Down in the frowst I heard them snore.
'Stand to!' Somebody grunted and swore.
 Dawn was misty; the skies were still;
 Larks were singing, discordant, shrill;
 They seemed happy; but *I* felt ill.
Deep in water I splashed my way
Up the trench to our bogged front line.
Rain had fallen the whole damned night.
O Jesus, send me a wound to-day,
And I'll believe in Your bread and wine,
And get my bloody old sins washed white!

The Choral Union

He staggered in from night and frost and fog
And lampless streets: he'd guzzled like a hog
And drunk till he was dazed. And now he came
To hear—he couldn't call to mind the name—

But he'd been given a ticket for the show,
And thought he'd (hiccup) chance his luck and go.

The hall swam in his eyes, and soaring light
Was dazzling splendid after the dank night.
He sat and blinked, safe in his cushioned seat,
And licked his lips; he'd like a brandy, neat.

'Who is the King of Glory?' they were saying,
He pricked his ears; what was it? Were they praying? . . .
By God, it might be Heaven! For singers stood
Ranked in pure white; and everyone seemed good;
And clergymen were sitting meekly round
With joyful faces, drinking in the sound;
And holy women, and plump whiskered men.
Could this be Heaven? And was he dead? And then
They all stood up; the mighty chorus broke
In storms of song above those blameless folk;
And 'Hallelujah, Hallelujah!' rang
The burden of the triumph that they sang.

He gasped; it *must* be true; he'd got to Heaven
With all his sins that seventy times were seven;
And whispering 'Hallelujah' mid their shout,
He wondered when Lord God would turn him out.

The One-Legged Man

Propped on a stick he viewed the August weald;
Squat orchard trees and oasts with painted cowls;

A homely, tangled hedge, a corn-stalked field,
And sound of barking dogs and farmyard fowls.

And he'd come home again to find it more
Desirable than ever it was before.
How right it seemed that he should reach the span
Of comfortable years allowed to man!
Splendid to eat and sleep and choose a wife,
Safe with his wound, a citizen of life.
He hobbled blithely through the garden gate,
And thought: 'Thank God they had to amputate!'

Enemies

He stood alone in some queer sunless place
Where Armageddon ends. Perhaps he longed
For days he might have lived; but his young face
Gazed forth untroubled: and suddenly there thronged
Round him the hulking Germans that I shot
When for his death my brooding rage was hot.

He stared at them, half-wondering; and then
They told him how I'd killed them for his sake—
Those patient, stupid, sullen ghosts of men;
And still there seemed no answer he could make.
At last he turned and smiled. One took his hand
Because his face could make them understand.

The Tombstone-Maker

He primmed his loose red mouth and leaned his head
Against a sorrowing angel's breast, and said:
'You'd think so much bereavement would have made
'Unusual big demands upon my trade.
'The War comes cruel hard on some poor folk;
'Unless the fighting stops I'll soon be broke.'

He eyed the Cemetery across the road.
'There's scores of bodies out abroad, this while,
'That should be here by rights. They little know'd
'How they'd get buried in such wretched style.'

I told him with a sympathetic grin,
That Germans boil dead soldiers down for fat;
And he was horrified. 'What shameful sin!
'O sir, that Christian souls should come to that!'

Arms and the Man

Young Croesus went to pay his call
On Colonel Sawbones, Caxton Hall:
And, though his wound was healed and mended,
He hoped he'd get his leave extended.

The waiting-room was dark and bare.
He eyed a neat-framed notice there
Above the fireplace hung to show
Disabled heroes where to go

For arms and legs; with scale of price,
And words of dignified advice
How officers could get them free.

Elbow or shoulder, hip or knee,
Two arms, two legs, though all were lost,
They'd be restored him free of cost.
Then a Girl Guide looked to say,
'Will Captain Croesus come this way?'

Died of Wounds

His wet white face and miserable eyes
Brought nurses to him more than groans and sighs:
But hoarse and low and rapid rose and fell
His troubled voice: he did the business well.

The ward grew dark; but he was still complaining
And calling out for 'Dickie'. 'Curse the Wood!
'It's time to go. O Christ, and what's the good?
'We'll never take it, and it's always raining.'

I wondered where he'd been; then heard him shout,
'They snipe like hell! O Dickie, don't go out' . . .
I fell asleep . . . Next morning he was dead;
And some Slight Wound lay smiling on the bed.

The Hero

— didn't understand son

'Jack fell as he'd have wished,' the Mother said,
And folded up the letter that she'd read.
'The Colonel writes so nicely.' Something broke
In the tired voice that quavered to a choke.
She half looked up. 'We mothers are so proud
Of our dead soldiers.' Then her face was bowed. ← *— doesn't really help*

Quietly the Brother Officer went out.
He'd told the poor old dear some gallant lies
That she would nourish all her days, no doubt. *let them grow*
For while he coughed and mumbled, her weak eyes
Had shone with gentle triumph, brimmed with joy, *— strange — tears?*
Because he'd been so brave, her glorious boy.

He thought how 'Jack', cold-footed, useless swine,
Had panicked down the trench that night the mine *— coward*
Went up at Wicked Corner; how he'd tried *soldiers attitude*
To get sent home, and how, at last, he died,
Blown to small bits. And no one seemed to care
Except that lonely woman with white hair.

Stretcher Case

He woke; the clank and racket of the train
Kept time with angry throbbings in his brain.
Then for a while he lapsed and drowsed again.

[29]

At last he lifted his bewildered eyes
And blinked, and rolled them sidelong; hills and skies,
Heavily wooded, hot with August haze,
And, slipping backward, golden for his gaze,
Acres of harvest.

             Feebly now he drags
Exhausted ego back from glooms and quags
And blasting tumult, terror, hurtling glare,
To calm and brightness, havens of sweet air.
He sighed, confused; then drew a cautious breath;
This level journeying was no ride through death.
'If I were dead,' he mused, 'there'd be no thinking—
Only some plunging underworld of sinking,
And hueless, shifting welter where I'd drown.'

Then he remembered that his name was Brown.

But was he back in Blighty? Slow he turned,
Till in his heart thanksgiving leapt and burned.
There shone the blue serene, the prosperous land,
Trees, cows and hedges; skipping these, he scanned
Large, friendly names, that change not with the year,
Lung Tonic, Mustard, Liver Pills and Beer.

Conscripts

'Fall in, that awkward squad, and strike no more
Attractive attitudes! Dress by the right!
The luminous rich colours that you wore
Have changed to hueless khaki in the night.

Magic? What's magic got to do with you?
There's no such thing! Blood's red, and skies are blue.'

They gasped and sweated, marching up and down.
I drilled them till they cursed my raucous shout.
Love chucked his lute away and dropped his crown.
Rhyme got sore heels and wanted to fall out.
'Left, right! Press on your butts!' They looked at me
Reproachful; how I longed to set them free!

I gave them lectures on Defence, Attack;
They fidgeted and shuffled, yawned and sighed,
And boggled at my questions. Joy was slack,
And Wisdom gnawed his fingers, gloomy-eyed.
Young Fancy—how I loved him all the while—
Stared at his note-book with a rueful smile.

Their training done, I shipped them all to France,
Where most of those I'd loved too well got killed.
Rapture and pale Enchantment and Romance,
And many a sickly, slender lord who'd filled
My soul long since with lutanies of sin,
Went home, because they couldn't stand the din.

But the kind, common ones that I despised
(Hardly a man of them I'd count as friend),
What stubborn-hearted virtues they disguised!
They stood and played the hero to the end,
Won gold and silver medals bright with bars,
And marched resplendent home with crowns and stars.

The Road

The road is thronged with women; soldiers pass
And halt, but never see them; yet they're here—
A patient crowd along the sodden grass,
Silent, worn out with waiting, sick with fear.
The road goes crawling up a long hillside,
All ruts and stones and sludge, and the emptied dregs
Of battle thrown in heaps. Here where they died
Are stretched big-bellied horses with stiff legs,
And dead men, bloody-fingered from the fight,
Stare up at caverned darkness winking white.

You in the bomb-scorched kilt, poor sprawling Jock,
You tottered here and fell, and stumbled on,
Half dazed for want of sleep. No dream would mock
Your reeling brain with comforts lost and gone.
You did not feel her arms about your knees,
Her blind caress, her lips upon your head.
Too tired for thoughts of home and love and ease,
The road would serve you well enough for bed.

Secret Music

I keep such music in my brain
No din this side of death can quell;
Glory exulting over pain,
And beauty, garlanded in hell.

[32]

My dreaming spirit will not heed
The roar of guns that would destroy
My life that on the gloom can read
Proud-surging melodies of joy.

To the world's end I went, and found
Death in his carnival of glare;
But in my torment I was crowned,
And music dawned above despair.

Before the Battle

Music of whispering trees
Hushed by a broad-winged breeze
Where shaken water gleams;
And evening radiance falling
With reedy bird-notes calling.
O bear me safe through dark, you low-voiced streams.

I have no need to pray
That fear may pass away;
I scorn the growl and rumble of the fight
That summons me from cool
Silence of marsh and pool
And yellow lilies islanded in light.
O river of stars and shadows, lead me through the night.

June 25th, 1916.

The Death-Bed

He drowsed and was aware of silence heaped
Round him, unshaken as the steadfast walls;
Aqueous like floating rays of amber light,
Soaring and quivering in the wings of sleep.
Silence and safety; and his mortal shore
Lipped by the inward, moonless waves of death.

Someone was holding water to his mouth.
He swallowed, unresisting; moaned and dropped
Through crimson gloom to darkness; and forgot
The opiate throb and ache that was his wound.
   Water—calm, sliding green above the weir.
   Water—a sky-lit alley for his boat,
   Bird-voiced, and bordered with reflected flowers
   And shaken hues of summer; drifting down,
   He dipped contented oars, and sighed, and slept.

Night, with a gust of wind, was in the ward,
Blowing the curtain to a glimmering curve.
Night. He was blind; he could not see the stars
Glinting among the wraiths of wandering cloud;
Queer blots of colour, purple, scarlet, green,
Flickered and faded in his drowning eyes.

Rain—he could hear it rustling through the dark;
Fragrance and passionless music woven as one;
Warm rain on drooping roses; pattering showers
That soak the woods; not the harsh rain that sweeps
Behind the thunder, but a trickling peace,
Gently and slowly washing life away.

He stirred, shifting his body; then the pain
Leapt like a prowling beast, and gripped and tore
His groping dreams with grinding claws and fangs.
　　But someone was beside him; soon he lay
　　Shuddering because that evil thing had passed.
　　And death, who'd stepped toward him, paused and
　　　　stared.

Light many lamps and gather round his bed.
Lend him your eyes, warm blood, and will to live.
Speak to him; rouse him; you may save him yet.
He's young; he hated War; how should he die
When cruel old campaigners win safe through?

But death replied: 'I choose him.' So he went,
And there was silence in the summer night;
Silence and safety; and the veils of sleep.
Then, far away, the thudding of the guns.

The Last Meeting

I

Because the night was falling warm and still
Upon a golden day at April's end,
I thought; I will go up the hill once more
To find the face of him that I have lost,
And speak with him before his ghost has flown
Far from the earth that might not keep him long.

[35]

So down the road I went, pausing to see
How slow the dusk drew on, and how the folk
Loitered about their doorways, well-content
With the fine weather and the waxing year.
The miller's house, that glimmered with grey walls,
Turned me aside; and for a while I leaned
Along the tottering rail beside the bridge
To watch the dripping mill-wheel green with damp.
The miller peered at me with shadowed eyes
And pallid face: I could not hear his voice
For sound of the weir's plunging. He was old.
His days went round with the unhurrying wheel.

Moving along the street, each side I saw
The humble, kindly folk in lamp-lit rooms;
Children at table; simple, homely wives;
Strong, grizzled men; and soldiers back from war,
Scaring the gaping elders with loud talk.

Soon all the jumbled roofs were down the hill,
And I was turning up the grassy lane
That goes to the big, empty house that stands
Above the town, half-hid by towering trees.
I looked below and saw the glinting lights:
I heard the treble cries of bustling life,
And mirth, and scolding; and the grind of wheels.
An engine whistled, piercing-shrill, and called
High echoes from the sombre slopes afar;
Then a long line of trucks began to move.

It was quite still; the columned chestnuts stood
Dark in their noble canopies of leaves.

I thought: 'A little longer I'll delay,
And then he'll be more glad to hear my feet,
And with low laughter ask me why I'm late.
The place will be too dim to show his eyes,
But he will loom above me like a tree,
With lifted arms and body tall and strong.'

There stood the empty house; a ghostly hulk
Becalmed and huge, massed in the mantling dark,
As builders left it when quick-shattering war
Leapt upon France and called her men to fight.
Lightly along the terraces I trod,
Crunching the rubble till I found the door
That gaped in twilight, framing inward gloom.
An owl flew out from under the high eaves
To vanish secretly among the firs,
Where lofty boughs netted the gleam of stars.
I stumbled in; the dusty floors were strewn
With cumbering piles of planks and props and beams;
Tall windows gapped the walls; the place was free
To every searching gust and jousting gale;
But now they slept; I was afraid to speak,
And heavily the shadows crowded in.

I called him, once; then listened: nothing moved:
Only my thumping heart beat out the time.
Whispering his name, I groped from room to room.

Quite empty was that house; it could not hold
His human ghost, remembered in the love
That strove in vain to be companioned still.

Blindly I sought the woods that I had known
So beautiful with morning when I came
Amazed with spring that wove the hazel twigs
With misty raiment of awakening green.
I found a holy dimness, and the peace
Of sanctuary, austerely built of trees,
And wonder stooping from the tranquil sky.

Ah! but there was no need to call his name.
He was beside me now, as swift as light.
I knew him crushed to earth in scentless flowers,
And lifted in the rapture of dark pines.
'For now,' he said, 'my spirit has more eyes
Than heaven has stars; and they are lit by love.
My body is the magic of the world,
And dawn and sunset flame with my spilt blood.
My breath is the great wind, and I am filled
With molten power and surge of the bright waves
That chant my doom along the ocean's edge.

'Look in the faces of the flowers and find
The innocence that shrives me; stoop to the stream
That you may share the wisdom of my peace.
For talking water travels undismayed.
The luminous willows lean to it with tales
Of the young earth; and swallows dip their wings
Where showering hawthorn strews the lanes of light.

'I can remember summer in one thought
Of wind-swept green, and deeps of melting blue,
And scent of limes in bloom; and I can hear

Distinct the early mower in the grass,
Whetting his blade along some morn of June.

'For I was born to the round world's delight,
And knowledge of enfolding motherhood,
Whose tenderness, that shines through constant toil,
Gathers the naked children to her knees.
In death I can remember how she came
To kiss me while I slept; still I can share
The glee of childhood; and the fleeting gloom
When all my flowers were washed with rain of tears.

'I triumph in the choruses of birds,
Bursting like April buds in gyres of song.
My meditations are the blaze of noon
On silent woods, where glory burns the leaves.
I have shared breathless vigils; I have slaked
The thirst of my desires in bounteous rain
Pouring and splashing downward through the dark.
Loud storm has roused me with its winking glare,
And voice of doom that crackles overhead.
I have been tired and watchful, craving rest,
Till the slow-footed hours have touched my brows
And laid me on the breast of sundering sleep.'

III

I know that he is lost among the stars,
And may return no more but in their light.
Though his hushed voice may call me in the stir
Of whispering trees, I shall not understand.

Men may not speak with stillness; and the joy
Of brooks that leap and tumble down green hills
Is faster than their feet; and all their thoughts
Can win no meaning from the talk of birds.

My heart is fooled with fancies, being wise;
For fancy is the gleaming of wet flowers
When the hid sun looks forth with golden stare.
Thus, when I find new loveliness to praise,
And things long-known shine out in sudden grace,
Then will I think: 'He moves before me now.'
So he will never come but in delight,
And, as it was in life, his name shall be
Wonder awaking in a summer dawn,
And youth, that dying, touched my lips to song.

Flixécourt. May 1916.

A Letter Home

I

Here I'm sitting in the gloom
Of my quiet attic room.
France goes rolling all around,
Fledged with forest May has crowned.
And I puff my pipe, calm-hearted,
Thinking how the fighting started,
Wondering when we'll ever end it,
Back to Hell with Kaiser send it,

Gag the noise, pack up and go,
Clockwork soldiers in a row.
I've got better things to do
Than to waste my time on you.

2

Robert, when I drowse to-night,
Skirting lawns of sleep to chase
Shifting dreams in mazy light,
Somewhere then I'll see your face
Turning back to bid me follow
Where I wag my arms and hollo,
Over hedges hasting after
Crooked smile and baffling laughter.
   Running tireless, floating, leaping,
   Down your web-hung woods and valleys,
   Garden glooms and hornbeam alleys,
   Where the glowworm stars are peeping,
   Till I find you, quiet as stone
   On a hill-top all alone,
   Staring outward, gravely pondering
   Jumbled leagues of hillock-wandering.

3

You and I have walked together
In the starving winter weather.
We've been glad because we knew
Time's too short and friends are few.
We've been sad because we missed
One whose yellow head was kissed

By the gods, who thought about him
Till they couldn't do without him.
Now he's here again; I've seen
Soldier David dressed in green,
Standing in a wood that swings
To the madrigal he sings.
He's come back, all mirth and glory,
Like the prince in fairy story.
Winter called him far away;
Blossoms bring him home with May.

4

Well, I know you'll swear it's true
That you found him decked in blue
Striding up through morning-land
With a cloud on either hand.
Out in Wales, you'll say, he marches,
Arm in arm with oaks and larches;
Hides all night in hilly nooks,
Laughs at dawn in tumbling brooks.
    Yet, it's certain, here he teaches
    Outpost-schemes to groups of beeches.
    And I'm sure, as here I stand,
    That he shines through every land,
    That he sings in every place
    Where we're thinking of his face.

5

Robert, there's a war in France;
Everywhere men bang and blunder,

[42]

Sweat and swear and worship Chance,
Creep and blink through cannon thunder.
Rifles crack and bullets flick,
Sing and hum like hornet-swarms.
Bones are smashed and buried quick.
   Yet, through stunning battle storms,
   All the while I watch the spark
   Lit to guide me; for I know
   Dreams will triumph, though the dark
   Scowls above me where I go.
You can hear me; you can mingle
Radiant folly with my jingle.
War's a joke for me and you
While we know such dreams are true!

S.S. Flixécourt. May 1916.

III

LYRICAL POEMS: 1908-16

Nimrod in September

When half the drowsy world's a-bed
And misty morning rises red,
With jollity of horn and lusty cheer,
Young Nimrod urges on his dwindling rout;
Along the yellowing coverts we can hear
His horse's hoofs thud hither and about:
In mulberry coat he rides and makes
Huge clamour in the sultry brakes.

Morning Express

Along the wind-swept platform, pinched and white,
The travellers stand in pools of wintry light,
Offering themselves to morn's long, slanting arrows.
The train's due; porters trundle laden barrows.
The train steams in, volleying resplendent clouds
Of sun-blown vapour. Hither and about,
Scared people hurry, storming the doors in crowds.
The officials seem to waken with a shout,
Resolved to hoist and plunder; some to the vans
Leap; others rumble the milk in gleaming cans.

Boys, indolent-eyed, from baskets leaning back,
Question each face; a man with a hammer steals
Stooping from coach to coach; with clang and clack
Touches and tests, and listens to the wheels.
Guard sounds a warning whistle, points to the clock
With brandished flag, and on his folded flock
Claps the last door: the monster grunts: 'Enough!'
Tightening his load of links with pant and puff.
Under the arch, then forth into blue day,
Glide the processional windows on their way,
And glimpse the stately folk who sit at ease
To view the world like kings taking the seas
In prosperous weather: drifting banners tell
Their progress to the counties; with them goes
The clamour of their journeying; while those
Who sped them stand to wave a last farewell.

Noah

When old Noah stared across the floods,
Sky and water melted into one
Looking-glass of shifting tides and sun.

Mountain-tops were few: the ship was foul:
All the morn old Noah marvelled greatly
At this weltering world that shone so stately,
Drowning deep the rivers and the plains.
Through the stillness came a rippling breeze;
Noah sighed, remembering the green trees.

[45]

Clear along the morning stooped a bird,—
Lit beside him with a blossomed sprig.
Earth was saved; and Noah danced a jig.

David Cleek

I cannot think that Death will press his claim
To snuff you out or put you off your game:
You'll still contrive to play your steady round,
Though hurricanes may sweep the dismal ground,
And darkness blur the sandy-skirted green
Where silence gulfs the shot you strike so clean.

Saint Andrew guard your ghost, old David Cleek,
And send you home to Fifeshire once a week!
Good fortune speed your ball upon its way
When Heaven decrees its mightiest Medal Day;
Till saints and angels hymn for evermore
The miracle of your astounding score;
And He who keeps all players in His sight,
Walking the royal and ancient hills of light
Standing benignant at the eighteenth hole,
To everlasting Golf consigns your soul.

Ancestors

Behold these jewelled, merchant Ancestors,
Foregathered in some chancellery of death;

Calm, provident, discreet, they stroke their beards
And move their faces slowly in the gloom,
And barter monstrous wealth with speech subdued,
Lustreless eyes and acquiescent lids.
    And oft in pauses of their conference,
    They listen to the measured breath of night's
    Hushed sweep of wind aloft the swaying trees
    In dimly gesturing gardens; then a voice
    Climbs with clear mortal song half-sad for heaven.

A silent-footed message flits and brings
The ghostly Sultan from his glimmering halls;
A shadow at the window, turbaned, vast,
He leans; and, pondering the sweet influence
That steals around him in remembered flowers,
Hears the frail music wind along the slopes,
Put forth, and fade across the whispering sea.

Haunted

Evening was in the wood, louring with storm.
A time of drought had sucked the weedy pool
And baked the channels; birds had done with song.
Thirst was a dream of fountains in the moon,
Or willow-music blown across the water
Leisurely sliding on by weir and mill.

Uneasy was the man who wandered, brooding,
His face a little whiter than the dusk.
A drone of sultry wings flicker'd in his head.

The end of sunset burning thro' the boughs
Died in a smear of red; exhausted hours
Cumber'd, and ugly sorrows hemmed him in.

He thought: 'Somewhere there's thunder,' as he strove
To shake off dread; he dared not look behind him,
But stood, the sweat of horror on his face.

He blunder'd down a path, trampling on thistles,
In sudden race to leave the ghostly trees.
And: 'Soon I'll be in open fields,' he thought,
And half remembered starlight on the meadows,
Scent of mown grass and voices of tired men,
Fading along the field-paths; home and sleep
And cool-swept upland spaces, whispering leaves,
And far off the long churring night-jar's note.

But something in the wood, trying to daunt him,
Led him confused in circles through the thicket.
He was forgetting his old wretched folly,
And freedom was his need; his throat was choking.
Barbed brambles gripped and clawed him round his legs,
And he floundered over snags and hidden stumps.
Mumbling: 'I will get out! I must get out!'
Butting and thrusting up the baffling gloom,
Pausing to listen in a space 'twixt thorns,
He peers around with peering, frantic eyes.

An evil creature in the twilight looping,
Flapped blindly in his face. Beating it off,
He screeched in terror, and straightway something
    clambered

Heavily from an oak, and dropped, bent double,
To shamble at him zigzag, squat and bestial.

Headlong he charges down the wood, and falls
With roaring brain—agony—the snap't spark—
And blots of green and purple in his eyes.
Then the slow fingers groping on his neck,
And at his heart the strangling clasp of death.

Blind

His headstrong thoughts that once in eager strife
Leapt sure from eye to brain and back to eye,
Weaving unconscious tapestries of life,
Are now thrust inward, dungeoned from the sky.
   And he who has watched his world and loved it all,
   Starless and old and blind, a sight for pity,
   With feeble steps and fingers on the wall,
   Gropes with his staff along the rumbling city.

Villon

They threw me from the gates: my matted hair
Was dank with dungeon wetness; my spent frame
O'erlaid with marish agues: everywhere
Tortured by leaping pangs of frost and flame,
So hideous was I that even Lazarus there
In noisome rags arrayed and leprous shame,
Beside me set had seemed full sweet and fair,
And looked on me with loathing.

                                        But one came
Who laid a cloak on me and brought me in
Tenderly to an hostel quiet and clean;
Used me with healing hands for all my needs.
The mortal stain of my reputed sin,
My state despised, and my defilèd weeds,
He hath put by as though they had not been.

Goblin Revel

In gold and grey, with fleering looks of sin,
I watch them come; by two, by three, by four,
Advancing slow, with loutings they begin
Their woven measure, widening from the door;
While music-men behind are straddling in
With flutes to brisk their feet across the floor,—
And jangled dulcimers, and fiddles thin
That taunt the twirling antic through once more.

They pause, and hushed to whispers, steal away.
With cunning glances; silent go their shoon
On creakless stairs; but far away the dogs
Bark at some lonely farm: and haply they
Have clambered back into the dusky moon
That sinks beyond the marshes loud with frogs.

Night-Piece

Ye hooded witches, baleful shapes that moan,
Quench your fantastic lanterns and be still;
For now the moon through heaven sails alone,
Shedding her peaceful rays from hill to hill.
The faun from out his dim and secret place
Draws nigh the darkling pool and from his dream
Half-wakens, seeing there his sylvan face
Reflected, and the wistful eyes that gleam.

To his cold lips he sets the pipe to blow
Some drowsy note that charms the listening air:
The dryads from their trees come down and creep
Near to his side; monotonous and low,
He plays and plays till at the woodside there
Stirs to the voice of everlasting sleep.

A Wanderer

When Watkin shifts the burden of his cares
And all that irked him in his bound employ,
Once more become a vagrom-hearted boy,
He moves to roundelays and jocund airs;
Loitering with dusty harvestmen, he shares
Old ale and sunshine; or, with maids half-coy,
Pays court to shadows; fools himself with joy,
Shaking a leg at junketings and fairs.

Sometimes, returning down his breezy miles,
A snatch of wayward April he will bring,
Piping the daffodilly that beguiles
Foolhardy lovers in the surge of spring.
And then once more by lanes and field-path stiles
Up the green world he wanders like a king.

October

Across the land a faint blue veil of mist
Seems hung; the woods wear yet arrayment sober
Till frost shall make them flame; silent and whist
The drooping cherry orchards of October
Like mournful pennons hang their shrivelling leaves
Russet and orange: all things now decay;
Long since ye garnered in your autumn sheaves,
And sad the robins pipe at set of day.

Now do ye dream of Spring when greening shaws
Confer with the shrewd breezes, and of slopes
Flower-kirtled, and of April, virgin guest;
Days that ye love, despite their windy flaws,
Since they are woven with all joys and hopes
Whereof ye nevermore shall be possessed.

The Heritage

Cry out on Time that he may take away
Your cold philosophies that give no hint

Of spirit-quickened flesh; fall down and pray
That Death come never with a face of flint:
Death is our heritage; with Life we share
The sunlight that must own his darkening hour:
Within his very presence yet we dare
To gather gladness like a fading flower.

For even as this, our joy not long may live
Perfect; and most in change the heart can trace
The miracle of life and human things:
All we have held to destiny we give;
Dawn glimmers on the soul-forsaken face;
Not we, but others, hear the bird that sings.

An Old French Poet

When in your sober mood my body have ye laid
In sight and sound of things beloved, woodland and
    stream,
And the green turf has hidden the poor bones ye deem
No more a close companion with those rhymes we made;

Then, if some bird should pipe, or breezes stir the glade,
Thinking them for the while my voice, so let them seem
A fading message from the misty shores of dream,
Or wheresoever, following Death, my feet have strayed.

Dryads

When meadows are grey with the morn
    In the dusk of the woods it is night:
The oak and the birch and the pine
    War with the glimmer of light.

Dryads brown as the leaf
    Move in the gloom of the glade;
When meadows are grey with the morn
    Dim night in the wood has delayed.

The cocks that crow to the land
    Are faint and hollow and shrill:
Dryads brown as the leaf
    Whisper, and hide, and are still.

Morning-Land

Old English songs, you bring to me
A simple sweetness somewhat kin
To birds that through the mystery
Of earliest morn make tuneful din,
While hamlet steeples sleepily
At cock-crow chime out three and four,
Till maids get up betime and go
With faces like the red sun low
Clattering about the dairy floor.

[54]

Arcady Unheeding

Shepherds go whistling on their way
In the spring season of the year;
One watches weather-signs of day;
One of his maid most dear
Dreams; and they do not hear
The birds that sing and sing; they do not see
Wide wealds of blue beyond their windy lea,
Nor blossoms red and white on every tree.

At Daybreak

I listen for him through the rain,
And in the dusk of starless hours
I know that he will come again;
Loth was he ever to forsake me:
He comes with glimmering of flowers
And stir of music to awake me.

Spirit of purity, he stands
As once he lived in charm and grace:
I may not hold him with my hands,
Nor bid him stay to heal my sorrow;
Only his fair, unshadowed face
Abides with me until to-morrow.

Dream-Forest

Where sunshine flecks the green,
Through towering woods my way
Goes winding all the day.

Scant are the flowers that bloom
Beneath the bosky screen
And cage of golden gloom.
Few are the birds that call,
Shrill-voiced and seldom seen.

Where silence masters all,
And light my footsteps fall,
The whispering runnels only
With blazing noon confer;
And comes no breeze to stir
The tangled thickets lonely.

A Child's Prayer

For Morn, my dome of blue,
For Meadows, green and gay,
And Birds who love the twilight of the leaves,
Let Jesus keep me joyful when I pray.

For the big Bees that hum
And hide in bells of flowers;
For the winding roads that come
To Evening's holy door,

May Jesus bring me grateful to his arms,
And guard my innocence for evermore.

Morning-Glory

In this meadow starred with spring
Shepherds kneel before their king.
Mary throned, with dreaming eyes,
Gowned in blue like rain-washed skies,
Lifts her tiny son that he
May behold their courtesy.
And green-smocked children, awed and good,
Bring him blossoms from the wood..

Clear the sunlit steeples chime
Mary's coronation-time.
Loud the happy children quire
To the golden-windowed morn;
While the lord of their desire
Sleeps below the crimson thorn.

To-day

This is To-day, a child in white and blue
Running to meet me out of Night who stilled
The ghost of Yester-eve; this is fair Morn
The mother of To-morrow. And these clouds
That chase the sunshine over gleaming hills
Are thoughts, delighting in the golden change
And the ceremony of their drifting state.

This is To-day. To-morrow might bring death,—
And Life, the gleeful madrigal of birds,
Be drowned in glimmer of sleep. To-day I know
How sweet it is to spend these eyes, and boast
This bubble of vistaed memory and sense
Blown by my joy aloft the glittering airs
Of heavenly peace. Oh take me to yourselves,
Earth, sky, and spirit! Let me stand within
The circle of your transience, that my voice
May thrill the lonely silences with song.

Wonderment

Then a wind blew;
And he who had forgot he moved
Lonely amid the green and silver morning weather,
Suddenly grew
Aware of clouds and trees
Gleaming and white and shafted, shaken together
And blown to music by the ruffling breeze.

Like flush of wings
The moment passed: he stood
Dazzled with blossom in the swaying wood;
Then he remembered how, through all swift things,
This mortal scene stands built of memories,—
Shaped by the wise
Who gazed in breathing wonderment,
And left us their brave eyes
To light the ways they went.

Daybreak in a Garden

I heard the farm cocks crowing, loud, and faint, and thin,
When hooded night was going and one clear planet
  winked:
I heard shrill notes begin down the spired wood distinct,
When cloudy shoals were chinked and gilt with fires of
  day.

 White-misted was the weald; the lawns were silver-
   grey;
 The lark his lonely field for heaven had forsaken;
 And the wind upon its way whispered the boughs of
   may,
 And touched the nodding peony-flowers to bid them
   waken.

Companions

Leave not your bough, my slender song-bird sweet,
But pipe me now your roundelay complete.

Come, gentle breeze, and tarrying on your way,
Whisper my trees what you have seen to-day.

Stand, golden cloud, until my song be done,
(For he's too proud) before the face of the sun.

So one did sing, and the other breathed a story;
Then both took wing, and the sun stepped forth in glory.

A Poplar and the Moon

There stood a Poplar, tall and straight;
The fair, round Moon, uprisen late,
Made the long shadow on the grass
A ghostly bridge 'twixt heaven and me.
  But May, with slumbrous nights, must pass;
  And blustering winds will strip the tree.
And I've no magic to express
The moment of that loveliness;
So from these words you'll never guess
The stars and lilies I could see.

South Wind

Where have you been, South Wind, this May-day
    morning,—
With larks aloft, or skimming with the swallow,
Or with blackbirds in a green, sun-glinted thicket?

Oh, I heard you like a tyrant in the valley;
Your ruffian haste shook the young, blossoming orchards;
You clapped rude hands, hallooing round the chimney,
And white your pennons streamed along the river.

You have robbed the bee, South Wind, in your adventure,
Blustering with gentle flowers; but I forgave you
When you stole to me shyly with scent of hawthorn.

Tree and Sky

Let my soul, a shining tree,
Silver branches lift towards thee,
Where on a hallowed winter's night
The clear-eyed angels may alight.

And if there should be tempests in
My spirit, let them surge like din
Of noble melodies at war;
With fervour of such blades of triumph as are
Flashed in white orisons of saints who go
On shafts of glory to the ecstasies they know.

Alone

I've listened: and all the sounds I heard
Were music,—wind, and stream, and bird.
With youth who sang from hill to hill
I've listened: my heart is hungry still.

I've looked: the morning world was green;
Bright roofs and towers of town I've seen;
And stars, wheeling through wingless night.
I've looked: and my soul yet longs for light.

I've thought: but in my sense survives
Only the impulse of those lives
That were my making. Hear me say
'I've thought!'—and darkness hides my day.

Storm and Sunlight

I

In barns we crouch, and under stacks of straw,
Harking the storm that rides a hurtling legion
Up the arched sky, and speeds quick heels of panic
With growling thunder loosed in fork and clap
That echoes crashing thro' the slumbrous vault.
　　The whispering woodlands darken: vulture Gloom
　　Stoops, menacing the skeltering flocks of Light,
　　Where the gaunt shepherd shakes his gleaming staff
　　And foots with angry tidings down the slope.
Drip, drip; the rain steals in through soaking thatch
By cob-webbed rafters to the dusty floor.
Drums shatter in the tumult; wrathful Chaos
Points pealing din to the zenith, then resolves
Terror in wonderment with rich collapse.

II

Now from drenched eaves a swallow darts to skim
The crystal stillness of an air unveiled
To tremulous blue. Raise your bowed heads, and let
Your horns adore the sky, ye patient kine!
Haste, flashing brooks! Small, chuckling rills, rejoice!
Be open-eyed for Heaven, ye pools of peace!
Shine, rain-bow hills! Dream on, fair glimpsèd vale
In haze of drifting gold! And all sweet birds,
Sing out your raptures to the radiant leaves!
And ye, close huddling Men, come forth to stand
A moment simple in the gaze of God

That sweeps along your pastures! Breathe his might!
Lift your blind faces to be filled with day,
And share his benediction with the flowers.

Wind in the Beechwood

The glorying forest shakes and swings with glancing
Of boughs that dip and strain; young, slanting sprays
Beckon and shift like lissom creatures dancing,
While the blown beechwood streams with drifting rays.
  Rooted in steadfast calm, grey stems are seen
  Like weather-beaten masts; the wood, unfurled,
  Seems as a ship with crowding sails of green
  That sweeps across the lonely billowing world.

O luminous and lovely! Let your flowers,
Your ageless-squadroned wings, your surge and gleam,
Drown me in quivering brightness: let me fade
  In the warm, rustling music of the hours
  That guard your ancient wisdom, till my dream
  Moves with the chant and whisper of the glade.

Wisdom

When Wisdom tells me that the world's a speck
Lost on the shoreless blue of God's To-Day . . .
I smile, and think, 'For every man his way:
The world's my ship, and I'm alone on deck!'

[63]

And when he tells me that the world's a spark
Lit in the whistling gloom of God's To-Night . . .
I look within me to the edge of dark,
And dream, 'The world's my field, and I'm the lark,
Alone with upward song, alone with light!'

Before Day

Come in this hour to set my spirit free
When earth is no more mine though night goes out,
And stretching forth these arms I cannot be
Lord of winged sunrise and dim Arcady:
When fieldward boys far off with clack and shout
From orchards scare the birds in sudden rout,
Come, ere my heart grows cold and full of doubt,
In the still summer dawns that waken me.

When the first lark goes up to look for day
And morning glimmers out of dreams, come then
Out of the songless valleys, over grey
Wide misty lands to bring me on my way:
For I am lone, a dweller among men
Hungered for what my heart shall never say.

COUNTER-ATTACK
AND
OTHER POEMS

Dans la trêve désolée de cette matinée, ces hommes qui avaient été tenaillés par la fatigue, fouettés par la pluie, bouleversés par toute une nuit de tonnerre, ces rescapés des volcans et de l'inondation entrevoyaient à quel point la guerre, aussi hideuse au moral qu'au physique, non seulement viole le bon sens, avilit les grandes idées, commande tous les crimes—mais ils se rappelaient combien elle avait développé en eux et autour d'eux tous les mauvais instincts sans en excepter un seul; la méchanceté jusqu'au sadisme, l'égoïsme jusqu'à la férocité, le besoin de jouir jusqu'à la folie.

HENRI BARBUSSE, *Le Feu*.

Prelude: The Troops

Dim, gradual thinning of the shapeless gloom
Shudders to drizzling daybreak that reveals
Disconsolate men who stamp their sodden boots
And turn dulled, sunken faces to the sky
Haggard and hopeless. They, who have beaten down
The stale despair of night, must now renew
Their desolation in the truce of dawn,
Murdering the livid hours that grope for peace.

Yet these, who cling to life with stubborn hands,
Can grin through storms of death and find a gap
In the clawed, cruel tangles of his defence.
They march from safety, and the bird-sung joy
Of grass-green thickets, to the land where all
Is ruin, and nothing blossoms but the sky
That hastens over them where they endure
Sad, smoking, flat horizons, reeking woods,
And foundered trench-lines volleying doom for doom.

O my brave brown companions, when your souls
Flock silently away, and the eyeless dead
Shame the wild beast of battle on the ridge,
Death will stand grieving in that field of war
Since your unvanquished hardihood is spent.
And through some mooned Valhalla there will pass
Battalions and battalions, scarred from hell;
The unreturning army that was youth;
The legions who have suffered and are dust.

Counter-Attack

We'd gained our first objective hours before
While dawn broke like a face with blinking eyes,
Pallid, unshaved and thirsty, blind with smoke.
Things seemed all right at first. We held their line,
With bombers posted, Lewis guns well placed,
And clink of shovels deepening the shallow trench.
     The place was rotten with dead; green clumsy legs
     High-booted, sprawled and grovelled along the saps
     And trunks, face downward, in the sucking mud,
     Wallowed like trodden sand-bags loosely filled;
     And naked sodden buttocks, mats of hair,
     Bulged, clotted heads slept in the plastering slime.
     And then the rain began,—the jolly old rain!

A yawning soldier knelt against the bank,
Staring across the morning blear with fog;
He wondered when the Allemands would get busy;
And then, of course, they started with five-nines
Traversing, sure as fate, and never a dud.
Mute in the clamour of shells he watched them burst
Spouting dark earth and wire with gusts from hell,
While posturing giants dissolved in drifts of smoke.
He crouched and flinched, dizzy with galloping fear,
Sick for escape,—loathing the strangled horror
And butchered, frantic gestures of the dead.

An officer came blundering down the trench:
'Stand-to and man the fire-step!' On he went . . .
Gasping and bawling, 'Fire-step . . . counter-attack!'

Then the haze lifted. Bombing on the right
Down the old sap: machine-guns on the left;
And stumbling figures looming out in front.
'O Christ, they're coming at us!' Bullets spat,
And he remembered his rifle . . . rapid fire . . .
And started blazing wildly . . . then a bang
Crumpled and spun him sideways, knocked him out
To grunt and wriggle: none heeded him; he choked
And fought the flapping veils of smothering gloom,
Lost in a blurred confusion of yells and groans . . .
Down, and down, and down, he sank and drowned,
Bleeding to death. The counter-attack had failed.

The Rear-Guard

(HINDENBURG LINE, APRIL 1917)

Groping along the tunnel, step by step,
He winked his prying torch with patching glare
From side to side, and sniffed the unwholesome air.

Tins, boxes, bottles, shapes too vague to know;
A mirror smashed, the mattress from a bed;
And he, exploring fifty feet below
The rosy gloom of battle overhead.

Tripping, he grabbed the wall; saw some one lie
Humped at his feet, half-hidden by a rug,
And stooped to give the sleeper's arm a tug.
'I'm looking for headquarters.' No reply.
'God blast your neck!' (For days he'd had no sleep,)
'Get up and guide me through this stinking place.'

[69]

Savage, he kicked a soft, unanswering heap,
And flashed his beam across the livid face
Terribly glaring up, whose eyes yet wore
Agony dying hard ten days before;
And fists of fingers clutched a blackening wound.

Alone he staggered on until he found
Dawn's ghost that filtered down a shafted stair
To the dazed, muttering creatures underground
Who hear the boom of shells in muffled sound.
At last, with sweat of horror in his hair,
He climbed through darkness to the twilight air,
Unloading hell behind him step by step.

Wirers

'Pass it along, the wiring party's going out'—
And yawning sentries mumble, 'Wirers going out.'
Unravelling; twisting; hammering stakes with muffled
    thud,
They toil with stealthy haste and anger in their blood.

The Boche sends up a flare. Black forms stand rigid there,
Stock-still like posts; then darkness, and the clumsy
        ghosts
Stride hither and thither, whispering, tripped by
        clutching snare
Of snags and tangles.
                    Ghastly dawn with vaporous coasts
Gleams desolate along the sky, night's misery ended.

Young Hughes was badly hit; I heard him carried away,
Moaning at every lurch; no doubt he'll die to-day.
But *we* can say the front-line wire's been safely mended.

Attack

At dawn the ridge emerges massed and dun
In the wild purple of the glow'ring sun,
Smouldering through spouts of drifting smoke that
     shroud
The menacing scarred slope; and, one by one,
Tanks creep and topple forward to the wire.
The barrage roars and lifts. Then, clumsily bowed
With bombs and guns and shovels and battle-gear,
Men jostle and climb to meet the bristling fire.
Lines of grey, muttering faces, masked with fear,
They leave their trenches, going over the top,
While time ticks blank and busy on their wrists,
And hope, with furtive eyes and grappling fists,
Flounders in mud. O Jesus, make it stop!

Dreamers

Soldiers are citizens of death's grey land,
     Drawing no dividend from time's to-morrows.
In the great hour of destiny they stand,
     Each with his feuds, and jealousies, and sorrows.
Soldiers are sworn to action; they must win
     Some flaming, fatal climax with their lives.

Soldiers are dreamers; when the guns begin
    They think of firelit homes, clean beds and wives.

I see them in foul dug-outs, gnawed by rats,
    And in the ruined trenches, lashed with rain,
Dreaming of things they did with balls and bats,
    And mocked by hopeless longing to regain
Bank-holidays, and picture shows, and spats,
    And going to the office in the train.

How to Die

Dark clouds are smouldering into red
    While down the craters morning burns.
The dying soldier shifts his head
    To watch the glory that returns;
He lifts his fingers toward the skies
    Where holy brightness breaks in flame;
Radiance reflected in his eyes,
    And on his lips a whispered name.

You'd think, to hear some people talk,
    That lads go West with sobs and curses,
And sullen faces white as chalk,
    Hankering for wreaths and tombs and hearses.
But they've been taught the way to do it
    Like Christian soldiers; not with haste
And shuddering groans; but passing through it
    With due regard for decent taste.

The Effect

'The effect of our bombardment was terrific. One man told me he had never seen so many dead before.'—*War Correspondent.*

'*He'd never seen so many dead before.*'
They sprawled in yellow daylight while he swore
And gasped and lugged his everlasting load
Of bombs along what once had been a road.
'*How peaceful are the dead.*'
Who put that silly gag in some one's head?

'*He'd never seen so many dead before.*'
The lilting words danced up and down his brain,
While corpses jumped and capered in the rain.
No, no; he wouldn't count them any more . . .
The dead have done with pain:
They've choked; they can't come back to life again.

When Dick was killed last week he looked like that,
Flapping along the fire-step like a fish,
After the blazing crump had knocked him flat . . .
'*How many dead? As many as ever you wish.*
Don't count 'em; they're too many.
Who'll buy my nice fresh corpses, two a penny?'

Twelve Months After

Hullo! here's my platoon, the lot I had last year.
'The war'll be over soon.'
                    'What 'opes?'
                                'No bloody fear!'
Then, 'Number Seven, 'shun! All present and correct.'
They're standing in the sun, impassive and erect.
Young Gibson with his grin; and Morgan, tired and
        white;
Jordan, who's out to win a D.C.M. some night;
And Hughes that's keen on wiring; and Davies ('79),
Who always must be firing at the Boche front line.

.   .   .   .   .

'Old soldiers never die; they simply fide a-why!'
That's what they used to sing along the roads last spring;
That's what they used to say before the push began;
That's where they are to-day, knocked over to a man.

The Fathers

Snug at the club two fathers sat,
Gross, goggle-eyed, and full of chat.
One of them said: 'My eldest lad
Writes cheery letters from Bagdad.
But Arthur's getting all the fun
At Arras with his nine-inch gun.'

'Yes,' wheezed the other, 'that's the luck!
My boy's quite broken-hearted, stuck

In England training all this year.
Still, if there's truth in what we hear,
The Huns intend to ask for more
    Before they bolt across the Rhine.'
I watched them toddle through the door—
    These impotent old friends of mine.

Base Details

If I were fierce, and bald, and short of breath,
    I'd live with scarlet Majors at the Base,
And speed glum heroes up the line to death.
    You'd see me with my puffy petulant face,
Guzzling and gulping in the best hotel,
    Reading the Roll of Honour. 'Poor young chap,'
I'd say—'I used to know his father well;
    Yes, we've lost heavily in this last scrap.'
And when the war is done and youth stone dead,
I'd toddle safely home and die—in bed.

The General

'Good-morning; good-morning!' the General said
When we met him last week on our way to the line.
Now the soldiers he smiled at are most of 'em dead,
And we're cursing his staff for incompetent swine.
'He's a cheery old card,' grunted Harry to Jack
As they slogged up to Arras with rifle and pack.

But he did for them both by his plan of attack.

Lamentations

I found him in the guard-room at the Base.
From the blind darkness I had heard his crying
And blundered in. With puzzled, patient face
A sergeant watched him; it was no good trying
To stop it; for he howled and beat his chest.
And, all because his brother had gone west,
Raved at the bleeding war; his rampant grief
Moaned, shouted, sobbed, and choked, while he was
      kneeling
Half-naked on the floor. In my belief
Such men have lost all patriotic feeling.

Does it Matter?

Does it matter?—losing your legs?...
For people will always be kind,
And you need not show that you mind
When the others come in after hunting
To gobble their muffins and eggs.

Does it matter?—losing your sight?...
There's such splendid work for the blind;
And people will always be kind,
As you sit on the terrace remembering
And turning your face to the light.

Do they matter?—those dreams from the pit?...
You can drink and forget and be glad,

And people won't say that you're mad;
For they'll know you've fought for your country
And no one will worry a bit.

Fight to a Finish

The boys came back. Bands played and flags were flying,
    And Yellow-Pressmen thronged the sunlit street
To cheer the soldiers who'd refrained from dying,
    And hear the music of returning feet.
'Of all the thrills and ardours War has brought,
This moment is the finest.' (So they thought.)

Snapping their bayonets on to charge the mob,
    Grim Fusiliers broke ranks with glint of steel,
At last the boys had found a cushy job.

    I heard the Yellow-Pressmen grunt and squeal;
And with my trusty bombers turned and went
To clear those Junkers out of Parliament.

Editorial Impressions

He seemed so certain 'all was going well',
As he discussed the glorious time he'd had
While visiting the trenches.
                            'One can tell
You've gathered big impressions!' grinned the lad
Who'd been severely wounded in the back

In some wiped-out impossible Attack.
'Impressions? Yes, most vivid! I am writing
A little book called *Europe on the Rack*,
Based on notes made while witnessing the fighting.
I hope I've caught the feeling of "the Line",
And the amazing spirit of the troops.
By Jove, those flying-chaps of ours are fine!
I watched one daring beggar looping loops,
Soaring and diving like some bird of prey.
And through it all I felt that splendour shine
Which makes us win.'
                        The soldier sipped his wine.
'Ah, yes, but it's the Press that leads the way!'

Suicide in the Trenches

I knew a simple soldier boy
Who grinned at life in empty joy,
Slept soundly through the lonesome dark,
And whistled early with the lark.

In winter trenches, cowed and glum,
With crumps and lice and lack of rum,
He put a bullet through his brain.
No one spoke of him again.

                    .

You smug-faced crowds with kindling eye
Who cheer when soldier lads march by,
Sneak home and pray you'll never know
The hell where youth and laughter go.

Glory of Women

You love us when we're heroes, home on leave,
Or wounded in a mentionable place.
You worship decorations; you believe
That chivalry redeems the war's disgrace.
You make us shells. You listen with delight,
By tales of dirt and danger fondly thrilled.
You crown our distant ardours while we fight,
And mourn our laurelled memories when we're killed.
You can't believe that British troops 'retire'
When hell's last horror breaks them, and they run,
Trampling the terrible corpses—blind with blood.
  O German mother dreaming by the fire,
  While you are knitting socks to send your son
  His face is trodden deeper in the mud.

Their Frailty

He's got a Blighty wound. He's safe; and then
  War's fine and bold and bright.
She can forget the doomed and prisoned men
  Who agonize and fight.

He's back in France. She loathes the listless strain
  And peril of his plight,
Beseeching Heaven to send him home again,
  She prays for peace each night.

Husbands and sons and lovers ; everywhere
   They die ; War bleeds us white
Mothers and wives and sweethearts,—they don't care
   So long as He's all right.

The Hawthorn Tree

Not much to me is yonder lane
   Where I go every day ;
But when there's been a shower of rain
   And hedge-birds whistle gay,
I know my lad that's out in France
   With fearsome things to see
Would give his eyes for just one glance
   At our white hawthorn tree.

Not much to me is yonder lane
   Where *he* so longs to tread :
But when there's been a shower of rain
I think I'll never weep again
   Until I've heard he's dead.

The Investiture

God with a Roll of Honour in His hand
Sits welcoming the heroes who have died,
While sorrowless angels ranked on either side
Stand easy in Elysium's meadow-land.

Then *you* come shyly through the garden gate,
Wearing a blood-soaked bandage on your head;
And God says something kind because you're dead,
And homesick, discontented with your fate.

If I were there we'd snowball Death with skulls;
Or ride away to hunt in Devil's Wood
With ghosts of puppies that we walked of old.
But you're alone; and solitude annuls
Our earthly jokes; and strangely wise and good
You roam forlorn along the streets of gold.

Trench Duty

Shaken from sleep, and numbed and scarce awake,
Out in the trench with three hours' watch to take,
I blunder through the splashing mirk; and then
Hear the gruff muttering voices of the men
Crouching in cabins candle-chinked with light.
Hark! There's the big bombardment on our right
Rumbling and bumping; and the dark's a glare
Of flickering horror in the sectors where
We raid the Boche; men waiting, stiff and chilled,
Or crawling on their bellies through the wire.
'What? Stretcher-bearers wanted? Some one killed?'
Five minutes ago I heard a sniper fire:
Why did he do it? . . . Starlight overhead—
Blank stars. I'm wide-awake; and some chap's dead.

Break of Day

There seemed a smell of autumn in the air
At the bleak end of night; he shivered there
In a dank, musty dug-out where he lay,
Legs wrapped in sand-bags,—lumps of chalk and clay
Spattering his face. Dry-mouthed, he thought, 'To-day
We start the damned attack; and, Lord knows why,
Zero's at nine; how bloody if I'm done in
Under the freedom of that morning sky!'
And then he coughed and dozed, cursing the din.

Was it the ghost of autumn in that smell
Of underground, or God's blank heart grown kind,
That sent a happy dream to him in hell?—
Where men are crushed like clods, and crawl to find
Some crater for their wretchedness; who lie
In outcast immolation, doomed to die
Far from clean things or any hope of cheer,
Cowed anger in their eyes, till darkness brims
And roars into their heads, and they can hear
Old childish talk, and tags of foolish hymns.

He sniffs the chilly air; (his dreaming starts),
He's riding in a dusty Sussex lane
In quiet September; slowly night departs;
And he's a living soul, absolved from pain.
Beyond the brambled fences where he goes
Are glimmering fields with harvest piled in sheaves,
And tree-tops dark against the stars grown pale;
Then, clear and shrill, a distant farm-cock crows;

And there's a wall of mist along the vale
Where willows shake their watery-sounding leaves,
He gazes on it all, and scarce believes
That earth is telling its old peaceful tale;
He thanks the blessed world that he was born . . .
Then, far away, a lonely note of the horn.

They're drawing the Big Wood! Unlatch the gate,
And set Golumpus going on the grass;
He knows the corner where it's best to wait
And hear the crashing woodland chorus pass;
The corner where old foxes make their track
To the Long Spinney; that's the place to be.
The bracken shakes below an ivied tree,
And then a cub looks out; and 'Tally-o-back!'
He bawls, and swings his thong with volleying crack,—
All the clean thrill of autumn in his blood,
And hunting surging through him like a flood
In joyous welcome from the untroubled past;
While the war drifts away, forgotten at last.

Now a red, sleepy sun above the rim
Of twilight stares along the quiet weald,
And the kind, simple country shines revealed
In solitudes of peace, no longer dim.
The old horse lifts his face and thanks the light,
Then stretches down his head to crop the green.
All things that he has loved are in his sight;
The places where his happiness has been
Are in his eyes, his heart, and they are good.

Hark! there's the horn: they're drawing the Big Wood.

To Any Dead Officer

Well, how are things in Heaven? I wish you'd say,
  Because I'd like to know that you're all right.
Tell me, have you found everlasting day,
  Or been sucked in by everlasting night?
For when I shut my eyes your face shows plain;
  I hear you make some cheery old remark—
I can rebuild you in my brain,
  Though you've gone out patrolling in the dark.

You hated tours of trenches; you were proud
  Of nothing more than having good years to spend;
Longed to get home and join the careless crowd
  Of chaps who work in peace with Time for friend.
That's all washed out now. You're beyond the wire:
  No earthly chance can send you crawling back;
You've finished with machine-gun fire—
  Knocked over in a hopeless dud-attack.

Somehow I always thought you'd get done in,
  Because you were so desperate keen to live:
You were all out to try and save your skin,
  Well knowing how much the world had got to give.
You joked at shells and talked the usual 'shop,'
  Stuck to your dirty job and did it fine:
With 'Jesus Christ! when *will* it stop?
  Three years . . . It's hell unless we break their line.'

So when they told me you'd been left for dead
  I wouldn't believe them, feeling it *must* be true.
Next week the bloody Roll of Honour said

[84]

'Wounded and missing'—(That's the thing to do
When lads are left in shell-holes dying slow,
    With nothing but blank sky and wounds that ache,
Moaning for water till they know
    It's night, and then it's not worth while to wake!)

Good-bye, old lad! Remember me to God,
    And tell Him that our Politicians swear
They won't give in till Prussian Rule's been trod
    Under the Heel of England . . . Are you there? . . .
Yes . . . and the War won't end for at least two years;
But we've got stacks of men . . . I'm blind with tears,
    Staring into the dark. Cheero!
I wish they'd killed you in a decent show.

Sick Leave

When I'm asleep, dreaming and lulled and warm,—
They come, the homeless ones, the noiseless dead.
While the dim charging breakers of the storm
Bellow and drone and rumble overhead,
Out of the gloom they gather about my bed.
    They whisper to my heart; their thoughts are mine.
    'Why are you here with all your watches ended?
    From Ypres to Frise we sought you in the Line.'
In bitter safety I awake, unfriended;
And while the dawn begins with slashing rain
I think of the Battalion in the mud.
'When are you going out to them again?
Are they not still your brothers through our blood?'

Banishment

I am banished from the patient men who fight
They smote my heart to pity, built my pride.
Shoulder to aching shoulder, side by side,
They trudged away from life's broad wealds of light.
Their wrongs were mine; and ever in my sight
They went arrayed in honour. But they died,—
Not one by one: and mutinous I cried
To those who sent them out into the night.

The darkness tells how vainly I have striven
To free them from the pit where they must dwell
In outcast gloom convulsed and jagged and riven
By grappling guns. Love drove me to rebel.
Love drives me back to grope with them through hell;
And in their tortured eyes I stand forgiven.

Song-Books of the War

In fifty years, when peace outshines
Remembrance of the battle lines,
Adventurous lads will sigh and cast
Proud looks upon the plundered past.
On summer morn or winter's night,
Their hearts will kindle for the fight,
Reading a snatch of soldier-song,
Savage and jaunty, fierce and strong;

And through the angry marching rhymes
Of blind regret and haggard mirth,
They'll envy us the dazzling times
When sacrifice absolved our earth.

Some ancient man with silver locks
Will lift his weary face to say:
'War was a fiend who stopped our clocks
Although we met him grim and gay.'
And then he'll speak of Haig's last drive,
Marvelling that any came alive
Out of the shambles that men built
And smashed, to cleanse the world of guilt.
But the boys, with grin and sidelong glance,
Will think, 'Poor grandad's day is done.'
And dream of lads who fought in France
And lived in time to share the fun.

Thrushes

Tossed on the glittering air they soar and skim,
Whose voices make the emptiness of light
A windy palace. Quavering from the brim
Of dawn, and bold with song at edge of night,
They clutch their leafy pinnacles and sing
Scornful of man, and from his toils aloof
Whose heart's a haunted woodland whispering;
Whose thoughts return on tempest-baffled wing;
Who hears the cry of God in everything,
And storms the gate of nothingness for proof.

Autumn

October's bellowing anger breaks and cleaves
The bronzed battalions of the stricken wood
In whose lament I hear a voice that grieves
For battle's fruitless harvest, and the feud
Of outraged men. Their lives are like the leaves
Scattered in flocks of ruin, tossed and blown
Along the westering furnace flaring red.
O martyred youth and manhood overthrown,
The burden of your wrongs is on my head.

Invocation

Come down from heaven to meet me when my breath
Chokes, and through drumming shafts of stifling death
I stumble toward escape, to find the door
Opening on morn where I may breathe once more
Clear cock-crow airs across some valley dim
With whispering trees. While dawn along the rim
Of night's horizon flows in lakes of fire,
Come down from heaven's bright hill, my song's desire.

Belov'd and faithful, teach my soul to wake
In glades deep-ranked with flowers that gleam and shake
And flock your paths with wonder. In your gaze
Show me the vanquished vigil of my days.
Mute in that golden silence hung with green,
Come down from heaven and bring me in your eyes
Remembrance of all beauty that has been,
And stillness from the pools of Paradise.

Repression of War Experience

Now light the candles; one; two; there's a moth;
What silly beggars they are to blunder in
And scorch their wings with glory, liquid flame—
No, no, not that,—it's bad to think of war,
When thoughts you've gagged all day come back to
      scare you;
And it's been proved that soldiers don't go mad
Unless they lose control of ugly thoughts
That drive them out to jabber among the trees.

Now light your pipe; look, what a steady hand.
Draw a deep breath; stop thinking; count fifteen,
And you're as right as rain . . .
                   Why won't it rain? . . .
I wish there'd be a thunder-storm to-night,
With bucketsful of water to sluice the dark,
And make the roses hang their dripping heads.
Books; what a jolly company they are,
Standing so quiet and patient on their shelves,
Dressed in dim brown, and black, and white, and green,
And every kind of colour. Which will you read?
Come on; O *do* read something; they're so wise.
I tell you all the wisdom of the world
Is waiting for you on those shelves; and yet
You sit and gnaw your nails, and let your pipe out,
And listen to the silence: on the ceiling
There's one big, dizzy moth that bumps and flutters;
And in the breathless air outside the house
The garden waits for something that delays.
There must be crowds of ghosts among the trees,—

Not people killed in battle,—they're in France,—
But horrible shapes in shrouds—old men who died
Slow, natural deaths,—old men with ugly souls,
Who wore their bodies out with nasty sins.

.   .   .   .   .

You're quiet and peaceful, summering safe at home;
You'd never think there was a bloody war on! . . .
O yes, you would . . . why, you can hear the guns.
Hark! Thud, thud, thud,—quite soft . . . they never
     cease—
Those whispering guns—O Christ, I want to go out
And screech at them to stop—I'm going crazy;
I'm going stark, staring mad because of the guns.

Survivors

No doubt they'll soon get well; the shock and strain
    Have caused their stammering, disconnected talk.
Of course they're 'longing to go out again,'—
    These boys with old, scared faces, learning to walk.
They'll soon forget their haunted nights; their cowed
    Subjection to the ghosts of friends who died,—
Their dreams that drip with murder; and they'll be
    proud
    Of glorious war that shatter'd all their pride . . .
Men who went out to battle, grim and glad;
Children, with eyes that hate you, broken and mad.

Craiglockart. October, 1917.

Joy-Bells

Ring your sweet bells; but let them be farewells
    To the green-vista'd gladness of the past
That changed us into soldiers; swing your bells
    To a joyful chime; but let it be the last.

What means this metal in windy belfries hung
    When guns are all our need? Dissolve these bells
Whose tones are tuned for peace: with martial tongue
    Let them cry doom and storm the sun with shells.

Bells are like fierce-browed prelates who proclaim
    That 'if our Lord returned He'd fight for *us*.'
So let our bells and bishops do the same,
    Shoulder to shoulder with the motor-bus.

Remorse

Lost in the swamp and welter of the pit,
He flounders off the duck-boards; only he knows
Each flash and spouting crash,—each instant lit
When gloom reveals the streaming rain. He goes
Heavily, blindly on. And, while he blunders,
'Could anything be worse than this?'—he wonders,
Remembering how he saw those Germans run,
Screaming for mercy among the stumps of trees:
Green-faced, they dodged and darted: there was one
Livid with terror, clutching at his knees . . .
Our chaps were sticking 'em like pigs . . . 'O hell!'
He thought—'there's things in war one dare not tell
Poor father sitting safe at home, who reads
Of dying heroes and their deathless deeds.'

Dead Musicians

I

From you, Beethoven, Bach, Mozart,
    The substance of my dreams took fire.
You built cathedrals in my heart,
    And lit my pinnacled desire.
You were the ardour and the bright
    Procession of my thoughts toward prayer.
You were the wrath of storm, the light
    On distant citadels aflare.

II

Great names, I cannot find you now
    In these loud years of youth that strives
Through doom toward peace: upon my brow
    I wear a wreath of banished lives.
You have no part with lads who fought
    And laughed and suffered at my side.
Your fugues and symphonies have brought
    No memory of my friends who died.

III

For when my brain is on their track,
In slangy speech I call them back.
With fox-trot tunes their ghosts I charm.
'Another little drink won't do us any harm.'
    I think of rag-time; a bit of rag-time;

And see their faces crowding round
To the sound of the syncopated beat.
They've got such jolly things to tell,
Home from hell with a Blighty wound so neat . . .

And so the song breaks off; and I'm alone.
They're dead . . . For God's sake stop that gramophone.

The Dream

I

Moonlight and dew-drenched blossom, and the scent
Of summer gardens; these can bring you all
Those dreams that in the starlit silence fall:
Sweet songs are full of odours.
                                    While I went
Last night in drizzling dusk along a lane,
I passed a squalid farm; from byre and midden
Came the rank smell that brought me once again
A dream of war that in the past was hidden.

II

Up a disconsolate straggling village street
I saw the tired troops trudge: I heard their feet.
The cheery Q.M.S. was there to meet
And guide our Company in . . .
                                    I watched them stumble
Into some crazy hovel, too beat to grumble;

Saw them file inward, slipping from their backs
Rifles, equipment, packs.
On filthy straw they sit in the gloom, each face
Bowed to patched, sodden boots they must unlace,
While the wind chills their sweat through chinks and
    cracks.

III

I'm looking at their blistered feet; young Jones
Stares up at me, mud-splashed and white and jaded;
Out of his eyes the morning light has faded.
Old soldiers with three winters in their bones
Puff their damp Woodbines, whistle, stretch their toes:
They can still grin at me, for each of 'em knows
That I'm as tired as they are . . .
                Can they guess
The secret burden that is always mine?—
Pride in their courage; pity for their distress;
And burning bitterness
That I must take them to the accursèd Line.

IV

I cannot hear their voices, but I see
Dim candles in the barn: they gulp their tea,
And soon they'll sleep like logs. Ten miles away
The battle winks and thuds in blundering strife.
And I must lead them nearer, day by day,
To the foul beast of war that bludgeons life.

In Barracks

The barrack-square, washed clean with rain,
Shines wet and wintry-grey and cold.
Young Fusiliers, strong-legged and bold,
March and wheel and march again.
The sun looks over the barrack gate,
Warm and white with glaring shine,
To watch the soldiers of the Line
That life has hired to fight with fate.

Fall out: the long parades are done.
Up comes the dark; down goes the sun.
The square is walled with windowed light.
Sleep well, you lusty Fusiliers;
Shut your brave eyes on sense and sight,
And banish from your dreamless ears
The bugle's dying notes that say,
'Another night; another day.'

Together

Splashing along the boggy woods all day,
And over brambled hedge and holding clay,
I shall not think of him:
But when the watery fields grow brown and dim,
And hounds have lost their fox, and horses tire,
I know that he'll be with me on my way
Home through the darkness to the evening fire.

He's jumped each stile along the glistening lanes;
His hand will be upon the mud-soaked reins;
Hearing the saddle creak,
He'll wonder if the frost will come next week.
I shall forget him in the morning light;
And while we gallop on he will not speak:
But at the stable-door he'll say good-night.

PICTURE-SHOW

Picture-Show

And still they come and go: and this is all I know—
That from the gloom I watch an endless picture-show,
Where wild or listless faces flicker on their way,
With glad or grievous hearts I'll never understand
Because Time spins so fast, and they've no time to stay
Beyond the moment's gesture of a lifted hand.

And still, between the shadow and the blinding flame,
The brave despair of men flings onward, ever the same
As in those doom-lit years that wait them, and have
     been . . .
And life is just the picture dancing on a screen.

Reconciliation

When you are standing at your hero's grave,
Or near some homeless village where he died,
Remember, through your heart's rekindling pride,
The German soldiers who were loyal and brave.

Men fought like brutes; and hideous things were done;
And you have nourished hatred, harsh and blind.
But in that Golgotha perhaps you'll find
The mothers of the men who killed your son.

November 1918.

[99]

Concert Party

They are gathering round . . . .
Out of the twilight; over the grey-blue sand,
Shoals of low-jargoning men drift inward to the sound—
The jangle and throb of a piano . . . tum-ti-tum . . .
Drawn by a lamp, they come
Out of the glimmering lines of their tents, over the
      shuffling sand.

O sing us the songs, the songs of our own land,
You warbling ladies in white.
Dimness conceals the hunger in our faces,
This wall of faces risen out of the night,
These eyes that keep their memories of the places
So long beyond their sight.

Jaded and gay, the ladies sing; and the chap in brown
Tilts his grey hat; jaunty and lean and pale,
He rattles the keys . . . some actor-bloke from town . . .
God send you home; and then *A long, long trail*;
I hear you calling me; and *Dixieland* . . . .
Sing slowly . . . now the chorus . . . one by one
We hear them, drink them; till the concert's done.
Silent, I watch the shadowy mass of soldiers stand.
Silent, they drift away, over the glimmering sand.

Kantara, April 1918.

Night on the Convoy

(ALEXANDRIA-MARSEILLES)

Out in the blustering darkness, on the deck
A gleam of stars looks down. Long blurs of black,
The lean Destroyers, level with our track,
Plunging and stealing, watch the perilous way
Through backward racing seas and caverns of chill spray.
One sentry by the davits, in the gloom
Stands mute: the boat heaves onward through the
    night.
Shrouded is every chink of cabined light:
And sluiced by floundering waves that hiss and boom
And crash like guns, the troop-ship shudders . . .
    doom.

Now something at my feet stirs with a sigh;
And slowly growing used to groping dark,
I know that the hurricane-deck, down all its length,
Is heaped and spread with lads in sprawling strength—
Blanketed soldiers sleeping. In the stark
Danger of life at war, they lie so still,
All prostrate and defenceless, head by head . . .
And I remember Arras, and that hill
Where dumb with pain I stumbled among the dead.

We are going home. The troop-ship, in a thrill
Of fiery-chamber'd anguish, throbs and rolls.
We are going home . . . victims . . . three thousand souls.

May 1918.

The Dug-Out

Why do you lie with your legs ungainly huddled,
And one arm bent across your sullen, cold,
Exhausted face? It hurts my heart to watch you,
Deep-shadow'd from the candle's guttering gold;
And you wonder why I shake you by the shoulder;
Drowsy, you mumble and sigh and turn your head . . .
You are too young to fall asleep for ever;
And when you sleep you remind me of the dead.

St Venant, July 1918.

Battalion-Relief

'*Fall in! Now get a move on.*' (Curse the rain.)
We splash away along the straggling village,
Out to the flat rich country, green with June . . .
And sunset flares across wet crops and tillage,
Blazing with splendour-patches. (Harvest soon,
Up in the Line.) '*Perhaps the War'll be done*
'*By Christmas-Day. Keep smiling then, old son.*'

Here's the Canal: it's dusk; we cross the bridge.
'Lead on there, by platoons.' (The Line's a-glare
With shell-fire through the poplars; distant rattle
Of rifles and machine-guns.) '*Fritz is there!*
'*Christ, ain't it lively, Sergeant? Is't a battle?*'
More rain: the lightning blinks, and thunder rumbles.
'*There's over-head artillery!*' some chap grumbles.

[102]

What's all this mob at the cross-roads? Where are the
    guides? . . .
'Lead on with number One.' And off they go.
'Three minute intervals.' (Poor blundering files,
Sweating and blindly burdened; who's to know
If death will catch them in those two dark miles?)
More rain. 'Lead on, Head-quarters.' (That's the lot.)
'Who's that? . . . Oh, Sergeant-Major, don't get shot!
'And tell me, have we won this war or not?'

I Stood With the Dead

I stood with the Dead, so forsaken and still:
When dawn was grey I stood with the Dead.
And my slow heart said, 'You must kill, you must kill:
'Soldier, soldier, morning is red'.

On the shapes of the slain in their crumpled disgrace
I stared for a while through the thin cold rain . . .
'O lad that I loved, there is rain on your face,
'And your eyes are blurred and sick like the plain.'

I stood with the Dead . . . They were dead; they
    were dead;
My heart and my head beat a march of dismay:
And gusts of the wind came dulled by the guns.
'Fall in!' I shouted; 'Fall in for your pay!'

Memorial Tablet

(GREAT WAR)

Squire nagged and bullied till I went to fight,
(Under Lord Derby's Scheme). I died in hell—
(They called it Passchendaele). My wound was slight,
And I was hobbling back; and then a shell
Burst slick upon the duck-boards: so I fell
Into the bottomless mud, and lost the light.

At sermon-time, while Squire is in his pew,
He gives my gilded name a thoughtful stare;
For, though low down upon the list, I'm there;
'*In proud and glorious memory*' . . . that's my due.
Two bleeding years I fought in France, for Squire:
I suffered anguish that he's never guessed.
Once I came home on leave: and then went west . . .
What greater glory could a man desire?

To Leonide Massine in 'Cleopatra'

O beauty doomed and perfect for an hour,
Leaping along the verge of death and night,
You show me dauntless Youth that went to fight
Four long years past, discovering pride and power.

You die but in our dreams, who watch you fall
Knowing that to-morrow you will dance again.

[104]

But not to ebbing music were they slain
Who sleep in ruined graves, beyond recall;
Who, following phantom-glory, friend and foe,
Into the darkness that was War must go;
Blind; banished from desire.
                              O mortal heart
Be still; you have drained the cup; you have played your
      part.

Memory

When I was young my heart and head were light,
And I was gay and feckless as a colt
Out in the fields, with morning in the may,
Wind on the grass, wings in the orchard bloom.
    O thrilling sweet, my joy, when life was free
    And all the paths led on from hawthorn-time
    Across the carolling meadows into June.

But now my heart is heavy-laden. I sit
Burning my dreams away beside the fire:
For death has made me wise and bitter and strong;
And I am rich in all that I have lost.
    O starshine on the fields of long-ago,
    Bring me the darkness and the nightingale;
    Dim wealds of vanished summer, peace of home,
    And silence; and the faces of my friends.

To a Very Wise Man

I

Fires in the dark you build; tall quivering flames
In the huge midnight forest of the unknown.
Your soul is full of cities with dead names,
And blind-faced, earth-bound gods of bronze and stone
Whose priests and kings and lust-begotten lords
Watch the procession of their thundering hosts,
Or guard relentless fanes with flickering swords
And wizardry of ghosts.

II

In a strange house I woke; heard overhead
Hastily-thudding feet and a muffled scream . . .
(Is death like that?) . . . I quaked uncomforted,
Striving to frame to-morrow in a dream
Of woods and sliding pools and cloudless day.
(You know how bees come into a twilight room
From dazzling afternoon, then sail away
Out of the curtained gloom.)

III

You understand my thoughts; though, when *you* think,
You're out beyond the boundaries of my brain.
I'm but a bird at dawn that cries 'chink, chink'—
A garden-bird that warbles in the rain.
And you're the flying-man, the speck that steers
A careful course far down the verge of day,
Half-way across the world. Above the years
You soar . . . Is death so bad? . . . I wish you'd say.

Elegy

(TO ROBERT ROSS)

Your dextrous wit will haunt us long
Wounding our grief with yesterday.
Your laughter is a broken song;
And death has found you, kind and gay.

We may forget those transient things
That made your charm and our delight:
But loyal love has deathless wings
That rise and triumph out of night.

So, in the days to come, your name
Shall be as music that ascends
When honour turns a heart from shame . . .
O heart of hearts! . . . O friend of friends!

Miracles

I dreamt I saw a huge grey boat in silence steaming
Down a canal; it drew the dizzy landscape after;
The solemn world was sucked along with it—a streaming
Land-slide of loveliness. O, but I rocked with laughter,
Staring, and clinging to my tree-top. For a lake
Of gleaming peace swept on behind. (I mustn't wake.)

And then great clouds gathered and burst in spumes of
    green
That plunged into the water; and the sun came out

On glittering islands thronged with orchards scarlet-
    bloomed;
And rosy-plumed flamingoes flashed across the scene . . .
O, but the beauty of their freedom made me shout . . .
And when I woke I wondered where on earth I'd been.

The Goldsmith

'*This job's the best I've done.*' He bent his head
Over the golden vessel that he'd wrought.
A bird was singing. But the craftsman's thought
Is a forgotten language, lost and dead.

He sighed and stretch'd brown arms. His friend came in
And stood beside him in the morning sun.
The goldwork glitter'd. . . . '*That's the best I've done.*
'*And now I've got a necklace to begin.*'

This was at Gnossos, in the isle of Crete . . .
A girl was selling flowers along the street.

Devotion to Duty

I was near the King that day. I saw him snatch
And briskly scan the G.H.Q. dispatch.
Thick-voiced, he read it out. (His face was grave.)
'This officer advanced with the first wave,

'And when our first objective had been gained,
'(Though wounded twice), reorganized the line:
'The spirit of the troops was by his fine
'Example most effectively sustained.'

He gripped his beard; then closed his eyes and said,
'Bathsheba must be warned that he is dead.
'Send for her. I will be the first to tell
'This wife how her heroic husband fell.'

Ancient History

Adam, a brown old vulture in the rain,
Shivered below his wind-whipped olive-trees;
Huddling sharp chin on scarred and scraggy knees,
He moaned and mumbled to his darkening brain;
'*He was the grandest of them all—was Cain!*
'A lion laired in the hills, that none could tire;
'Swift as a stag; a stallion of the plain,
'Hungry and fierce with deeds of huge desire.'

Grimly he thought of Abel, soft and fair—
A lover with disaster in his face,
And scarlet blossom twisted in bright hair.
'Afraid to fight; was murder more disgrace?...
'*God always hated Cain*'... He bowed his head—
The gaunt wild man whose lovely sons were dead.

What the Captain said at the Point-to-Point

I've had a good bump round; my little horse
Refused the brook first time,
Then jumped it prime;
And ran out at the double,
But of course
There's always trouble at a double:
And then—I don't know how
It was—he turned it up
At that big, hairy fence before the plough;
And some young silly pup
(I don't know which),
Near as a toucher knocked me into the ditch;
But we finished full of running, and quite sound:
And anyhow I've had a good bump round.

Fancy Dress

Some Brave, awake in you to-night,
Knocked at your heart: an eagle's flight
Stirred in the feather on your head.
Your wide-set Indian eyes, alight
Above high cheek-bones smeared with red,
Unveiled cragg'd centuries, and led
You, the snared wraith of bygone things—
Wild ancestries of trackless Kings—
Out of the past . . . So men have felt
Strange anger move them as they knelt
Praying to gods serenely starred
In heavens where tomahawks are barred.

Middle-Ages

I heard a clash, and a cry,
And a horseman fleeing the wood.
The moon hid in a cloud.
Deep in shadow I stood.
'*Ugly work!*' thought I,
Holding my breath.
'*Men must be cruel and proud,*
'*Jousting for death*'.

With gusty glimmering shone
The moon; and the wind blew colder.
A man went over the hill,
Bent to his horse's shoulder.
'*Time for me to be gone*' . . .
Darkly I fled.
Owls in the wood were shrill,
And the moon sank red.

Butterflies

Frail Travellers, deftly flickering over the flowers;
O living flowers against the heedless blue
Of summer days, what sends them dancing through
This fiery-blossom'd revel of the hours?

Theirs are the musing silences between
The enraptured crying of shrill birds that make

Heaven in the wood while summer dawns awake;
And theirs the faintest winds that hush the green.

And they are as my soul that wings its way
Out of the starlit dimness into morn:
And they are as my tremulous being—born
To know but this, the phantom glare of day.

Wraiths

They know not the green leaves;
In whose earth-haunting dream
Dimly the forest heaves,
And voiceless goes the stream.
  Strangely they seek a place
  In love's night-memoried hall;
  Peering from face to face,
  Until some heart shall call
  And keep them, for a breath,
  Half-mortal . . . (*Hark to the rain!*) . . .
  They are dead . . . (*O hear how death
  Gropes on the shutter'd pane!*)

The Dark House

Dusk in the rain-soaked garden,
And dark the house within.
A door creaked: someone was early
To watch the dawn begin.

But he stole away like a thief
In the chilly, star-bright air:
Though the house was shuttered for slumber,
He had left one wakeful there.

Nothing moved in the garden.
Never a bird would sing,
Nor shake and scatter the dew from the boughs
With shy and startled wing.
But when that lover had passed the gate
A quavering thrush began . . .
'Come back; come back!' he shrilled to the heart
Of the passion-plighted man.

Idyll

In the grey summer garden I shall find you
With day-break and the morning hills behind you.
There will be rain-wet roses; stir of wings;
And down the wood a thrush that wakes and sings.
Not from the past you'll come, but from that deep
Where beauty murmurs to the soul asleep:
And I shall know the sense of life re-born
From dreams into the mystery of morn
Where gloom and brightness meet. And standing there
Till that calm song is done, at last we'll share
The league-spread, quiring symphonies that are
Joy in the world, and peace, and dawn's one star.

Parted

Sleepless I listen to the surge and drone
And drifting roar of the town's undertone;
Till through quiet falling rain I hear the bells
Tolling and chiming their brief tune that tells
Day's midnight end. And from the day that's over
No flashes of delight I can recover;
But only dreary winter streets, and faces
Of people moving in loud clanging places:
And I in my loneliness, longing for you . . .

For all I did to-day, and all I'll do
To-morrow, in this city of intense
Arteried activities that throb and strive,
Is but a beating down of that suspense
Which holds me from your arms.

                      I am alive
Only that I may find you at the end
Of these slow-striking hours I toil to spend,
Putting each one behind me, knowing but this—
That all my days are turning toward your kiss;
That all expectancy awaits the deep
Consoling passion of your eyes, that keep
Their radiance for my coming, and their peace
For when I find in you my love's release.

Lovers

You were glad to-night: and now you've gone away.
Flushed in the dark, you put your dreams to bed;
But as you fall asleep I hear you say
Those tired sweet drowsy words we left unsaid.

Sleep well: for I can follow you, to bless
And lull your distant beauty where you roam;
And with wild songs of hoarded loveliness
Recall you to these arms that were your home.

Slumber-Song

Sleep; and my song shall build about your bed
A paradise of dimness. You shall feel
The folding of tired wings; and peace will dwell
Throned in your silence: and one hour shall hold
Summer, and midnight, and immensity
Lulled to forgetfulness. For, where you dream,
The stately gloom of foliage shall embower
Your slumbering thought with tapestries of blue.
And there shall be no memory of the sky,
Nor sunlight with its cruelty of swords.
But, to your soul that sinks from deep to deep
Through drowned and glimmering colour, Time shall be
Only slow rhythmic swaying; and your breath;
And roses in the darkness; and my love.

The Imperfect Lover

I never asked you to be perfect—did I?—
Though often I've called you sweet, in the invasion
Of mastering love. I never prayed that you
Might stand, unsoiled, angelic and inhuman,
Pointing the way toward Sainthood like a sign-post.

Oh yes, I know the way to heaven was easy.
We found the little kingdom of our passion
That all can share who walk the road of lovers.
In wild and secret happiness we stumbled;
And gods and demons clamoured in our senses.

But I've grown thoughtful now. And you have lost
Your early-morning freshness of surprise
At being so utterly mine: you've learned to fear
The gloomy, stricken places in my soul,
And the occasional ghosts that haunt my gaze.

You made me glad; and I can still return
To you, the haven of my lonely pride:
But I am sworn to murder those illusions
That blossom from desire with desperate beauty:
And there shall be no falsehood in our failure;
Since, if we loved like beasts, the thing is done,
And I'll not hide it, though our heaven be hell.

You dream long liturgies of our devotion.
Yet, in my heart, I dread our love's destruction.
But, should you grow to hate me, I would ask

No mercy of your mood: I'd have you stand
And look me in the eyes, and laugh, and smite me.

Then I should know, at least, that truth endured,
Though love had died of wounds. And you could leave me
Unvanquished in my atmosphere of devils.

Vision

I love all things that pass: their briefness is
Music that fades on transient silences.
Winds, birds, and glittering leaves that flare and fall—
They fling delight across the world; they call
To rhythmic-flashing limbs that rove and race . . .
   A moment in the dawn for Youth's lit face;
   A moment's passion, closing on the cry—
   'O Beauty, born of lovely things that die!'

To a Childless Woman

You think I cannot understand. Ah, but I do . . .
I have been wrung with anger and compassion for you.
I wonder if you'd loathe my pity, if you knew.

But you *shall* know. I've carried in my heart too long
This secret burden. Has not silence wrought *your* wrong—
Brought you to dumb and wintry middle-age, with grey
Unfruitful withering?—Ah, the pitiless things I say . . .

What do you ask your God for, at the end of day,
Kneeling beside your bed with bowed and hopeless head?
What mercy can He give you?—Dreams of the unborn
Children that haunt your soul like loving words unsaid—
Dreams, as a song half-heard through sleep in early morn?

I see you in the chapel, where you bend before
The enhaloed calm of everlasting Motherhood
That wounds your life; I see you humbled to adore
The painted miracle you've never understood.

Tender, and bitter-sweet, and shy, I've watched you
        holding
Another's child. O childless woman, was it then
That, with an instant's cry, your heart, made young
        again,
Was crucified for ever—those poor arms enfolding
The life, the consummation that had been denied you?
I too have longed for children. Ah, but you must not
        weep.
Something I have to whisper as I kneel beside you . . .
And you must pray for me before you fall asleep.

Aftermath

Have you forgotten yet? . . .
For the world's events have rumbled on since those
        gagged days,
Like traffic checked while at the crossing of city-ways:
And the haunted gap in your mind has filled with thoughts
        that flow

Like clouds in the lit heaven of life ; and you're a man
    reprieved to go,
Taking your peaceful share of Time, with joy to spare.
But the past is just the same—and War's a bloody game . . .
Have you forgotten yet? . . .
Look down, and swear by the slain of the War that you'll never
    forget.

Do you remember the dark months you held the sector at
    Mametz—
The nights you watched and wired and dug and piled
    sandbags on parapets ?
Do you remember the rats ; and the stench
Of corpses rotting in front of the front-line trench—
And dawn coming, dirty-white, and chill with a hopeless
    rain ?
Do you ever stop and ask, 'Is it all going to happen again ?'

Do you remember that hour of din before the attack—
And the anger, the blind compassion that seized and
    shook you then
As you peered at the doomed and haggard faces of your
    men ?
Do you remember the stretcher-cases lurching back
With dying eyes and lolling heads—those ashen-grey
Masks of the lads who once were keen and kind and gay ?

Have you forgotten yet? . . .
Look up, and swear by the green of the spring that you'll never
    forget.

March 1919.

Prelude to an Unwritten Masterpiece

You like my bird-sung gardens: wings and flowers;
Calm landscapes for emotion; star-lit lawns;
And Youth against the sun-rise . . . *'Not profound;*
'But such a haunting music in the sound:
'Do it once more; it helps us to forget'.

Last night I dreamt an old recurring scene—
Some complex out of childhood; (sex, of course!)
I can't remember how the trouble starts;
And then I'm running blindly in the sun
Down the old orchard, and there's something cruel
Chasing me; someone roused to a grim pursuit
Of clumsy anger . . . Crash! I'm through the fence
And thrusting wildly down the wood that's dense
With woven green of safety; paths that wind
Moss-grown from glade to glade; and far behind,
One thwarted yell; then silence. I've escaped.

That's where it used to stop. Last night I went
Onward until the trees were dark and huge,
And I was lost, cut off from all return
By swamps and birdless jungles. I'd no chance
Of getting home for tea. I woke with shivers,
And thought of crocodiles in crawling rivers.

Some day I'll build (more ruggedly than Doughty)
A dark tremendous song you'll never hear.
My beard will be a snow-storm, drifting whiter
On bowed, prophetic shoulders, year by year.

And some will say, 'His work has grown so dreary.'
Others, 'He used to be a charming writer'.
And you, my friend, will query—
'Why can't you cut it short, you pompous blighter?'

Limitations

If you could crowd them into forty lines!
Yes; you can do it, once you get a start;
All that you want is waiting in your head,
For long-ago you've learnt it off by heart.

Begin: your mind's the room where you have slept,
(Don't pause for rhymes), till twilight woke you early.
The window stands wide-open, as it stood
When tree-tops loomed enchanted for a child
Hearing the dawn's first thrushes through the wood
Warbling (you know the words) serene and wild.

You've said it all before: you dreamed of Death,
A dim Apollo in the bird-voiced breeze
That drifts across the morning veiled with showers,
While golden weather shines among dark trees.

You've got your limitations; let them sing,
And all your life will waken with a cry:
Why should you halt when rapture's on the wing
And you've no limit but the cloud-flocked sky? . . .

But some chap shouts, 'Here, stop it; that's been done!'—
As God might holloa to the rising sun,
And then relent, because the glorying rays
Remind Him of green-glinting Eden days,
And Adam's trustful eyes as he looks up
From carving eagles on his beechwood cup.

Young Adam knew his job; he could condense
Life to an eagle from the unknown immense. . . .
Go on, whoever you are; your lines can be
A whisper in the music from the weirs
Of song that plunge and tumble toward the sea
That is the uncharted mercy of our tears.

                .   .

I told you it was easy! . . . Words are fools
Who follow blindly, once they get a lead.
But thoughts are kingfishers that haunt the pools
Of quiet; seldom-seen: and all you need
Is just that flash of joy above your dream.
So, when those forty platitudes are done,
You'll hear a bird-note calling from the stream
That wandered through your childhood; and the sun
Will strike the old flaming wonder from the waters. . . .
And there'll be forty lines not yet begun.

Falling Asleep

Voices moving about in the quiet house:
Thud of feet and a muffled shutting of doors:
Everyone yawning. Only the clocks are alert.

Out in the night there's autumn-smelling gloom
Crowded with whispering trees; across the park
A hollow cry of hounds like lonely bells:
And I know that the clouds are moving across the moon;
The low, red, rising moon. Now herons call
And wrangle by their pool; and hooting owls
Sail from the wood above pale stooks of oats.

Waiting for sleep, I drift from thoughts like these;
And where to-day was dream-like, build my dreams.
Music . . . there was a bright white room below,
And someone singing a song about a soldier,
One hour, two hours ago: and soon the song
Will be '*last night*': but now the beauty swings
Across my brain, ghost of remembered chords
Which still can make such radiance in my dream
That I can watch the marching of my soldiers,
And count their faces; faces; sunlit faces.

Falling asleep . . . the herons, and the hounds. . . .
September in the darkness; and the world
I've known; all fading past me into peace.

Everyone Sang

Everyone suddenly burst out singing;
And I was filled with such delight
As prisoned birds must find in freedom,
Winging wildly across the white
Orchards and dark-green fields; on—on—and out of
      sight.

Everyone's voice was suddenly lifted;
And beauty came like the setting sun:
My heart was shaken with tears; and horror
Drifted away . . . O, but Everyone
Was a bird; and the song was wordless; the singing will
      never be done.

SATIRICAL POEMS

Preface

Some say the Phœnix dwells in Aethiopia,
In Turkey, Syria, Tartary, or Utopia:
Others assume the continuance of the creature
In unexplored cosmographies of Nature:
One styles it Bird of Paradise; and one
Swears that its nest is built of cinnamon:
While sceptic Eastern Travellers would arraign
The existence of this paragon; and feign
That, since it seems so rare and unprolific,
The bird's a Pseudomorphous Hieroglyphic.

Afterthoughts on the Opening of the British Empire Exhibition

I muse by the midnight coals to the tick of a clock:
On pageants I ponder; I ask myself, 'What did it mean—
That ante-noontide ceremonial scene?'

I have sat in the Stadium, one face in a stabilized flock,
While the busbies and bayonets wheeled and took root on
    the green.
At the golden drum-majors I gazed; of the stands I took
    stock,

Till a roar rolled around the arena, from block after block,
Keeping pace with the carriage containing the King and
     the Queen.

Ebullitions of Empire exulted. I listened and stared.
Patriotic paradings with pygmy preciseness went by.
The band bashed out bandmaster music; the trumpeters
     blared.
The Press was collecting its clichés. (The cloud-covered
     sky
Struck a note of neutrality, extra-terrestrial and shy.)

The megaphone-microphone-magnified voice of the King
Spoke hollow and careful from vacant remoteness of air.
I heard. There was no doubt at all that the Sovereign was
     there;
He was there to be grave and august and to say the right
     thing;
To utter the aims of Dominion. He came to declare
An inaugurate Wembley. He did. Then a prelate, with
     prayer
To the God of Commercial Resources and Arts that are
     bland,
Was broadcasted likewise, his crozier of office in hand.
'For Thine is the Kingdom, the Power, and the Glory,'
     he said.

But when Elgar conducts the massed choirs something
     inward aspires;
For the words that they sing are by Blake; they are simple
     and grand,
And their rapture makes everything dim when the music
     has fled

And the guns boom salutes and the flags are unfurled
    overhead . . .
And the NAMES, the anonymous crowds, do they all
    understand?
Do they ask that their minds may be fierce for the lordship
    of light
Till in freedom and faith they have builded Jerusalem
    bright
For Empires and Ages remote from their war-memoried
    land?

On Reading the War Diary of a Defunct Ambassador

So that's your Diary—that's your private mind
Translated into shirt-sleeved History. That
Is what diplomacy has left behind
For after-ages to peruse, and find
What passed beneath your elegant silk-hat.

You were a fine old gentleman; compact
Of shrewdness, charm, refinement and finesse.
Impeccable in breeding, taste and dress,
No diplomatic quality you lacked—
No tittle of ambassadorial tact.

I can imagine you among 'the guns',
Urbanely peppering partridge, grouse, or pheasant—
Guest of those infinitely privileged ones
Whose lives are padded, petrified, and pleasant.

I visualize you feeding off gold plate
And gossiping on grave affairs of State.

Now you're defunct; your gossip's gravely printed;
The world discovers where you lunched and dined
On such and such a day; and what was hinted
By ministers and generals far behind
The all-important conflict, carnage-tinted.

The world can read the rumours that you gleaned
From various Fronts; the well-known Names you met;
Each conference you attended and convened;
And (at appropriate moments) what you ate.
Thus (if the world's acute) it can derive
Your self, exact, uncensored and alive.

The world will find no pity in your pages;
No exercise of spirit worthy of mention;
Only a public-funeral grief-convention;
And all the circumspection of the ages.
But I, for one, am grateful, overjoyed,
And unindignant that your punctual pen
Should have been so constructively employed
In manifesting to unprivileged men
The visionless officialized fatuity
That once kept Europe safe for Perpetuity.

Monody on the Demolition of
Devonshire House

Strolling one afternoon along a street
Whose valuable vastness can compare
With anything on earth in the complete
Efficiency of its mammoniac air—
Strolling (to put it plainly) through those bits
Of Londonment adjacent to the Ritz,
(While musing on the social gap between
Myself, whose arrogance is mostly brainy,
And those whose pride, on sunlit days and rainy,
Must loll and glide in yacht and limousine),
Something I saw, beyond a boarded barrier,
Which manifested well that Time's no tarrier.

Where stood the low-built mansion, once so great,
Ducal, demure, secure in its estate—
Where Byron rang the bell and limped upstairs,
And Lord knows what political affairs
Got muddled and remodelled while Their Graces
Manned unperturbed Elizabethan faces—
There, blankly overlooked by wintry strange
Frontage of houses rawly-lit by change,
Industrious workmen reconstructed quite
The lumbered, pegged, and excavated site;
And not one nook survived to screen a mouse
In what was Devonshire (God rest it) House.

Lines Written in Anticipation of a London Paper Attaining a Guaranteed Circulation of Ten Million Daily

So you have touched ten million! Well, I've noted
The annual increase of your circulation
From big to vast, from corpulent to bloated,
With, I confess, fastidious consternation.
But, as the saying goes, success succeeds;
And I'm now moved, as one who writes and reads,
To offer you my column of full-throated
(Though marketably dud) congratulation.

Ten million years at least this country lacked you.
Studying your antecedents I have tracked you
To someone Pleistocene whose cranium crudely
Began the upward biologic struggle,—
Some Harmsworth ancestor whose Public nudely
Conversed in jargon of guffaw and guggle.
(Who knows what yarns he told of his demeanour
When menaced by a mammoth cave-hyæna?)

Primeval days were dull. Events existed
As unexploited masses of material.
Wars, plagues, and famines functioned unassisted,
And there was no synopsis to the serial.
The Bible woke things up. Yes, from the start
That over-edited chronicle recorded
Stories engrossing to the human heart,
Sexual, sensational, topical, and sordid.
From Eden outwards, there was nothing lacking

But paper, print, a sound financial backing,
And an exploitable Public to peruse
A journalistic venture.
                    Have you thought—
(Allowing for the slackness of the Jews
In the promotion of athletic sport)—
What a real smart News Editor'd have done
With Mrs. Adam's anti-social slips?
Excogitate the head-lines he'd have run . . .
'*The Fall. Exclusive Story from Eve's Lips.*'
Then '*Public Barred from Eden.*' '*Cain Sheds Blood.*'
And '*Startling New Development of Flood.*'
And then the Gospels. . . . But why count the cost
Of unreported copy lived and lost?
The Past is an edition torn to tatters;
And only one thing now supremely matters;
Your enviable Journal's circulation
Exceeds our census'd London population.

But, while I write, doubt surges in my breast,
'To whom exactly are these words addressed?'
Do I so copiously congratulate
A lonely Earldom or a Syndicate?
Or am I speaking to familiar friends
Who hold your Shares and draw fat Dividends?
Were it not wiser, were it not more candid,
More courteous, more consistent with good sense,
If I were to include all, all who are banded
Together in achievement so immense?
For such inclusion is to have augmented
My audience to an almost national size.
I must congratulate those well-contented

And public-spirited Firms who advertise
Their functions, their ideals, their whole existence,
Across the current acreage of your sheets
With privileged and opulent persistence.
I must congratulate the London streets
Which you adorn with posters that reveal
From day to day, from hour to hour, those many
Events which most concern the public-weal,
And catch most easily the public-penny.
I must congratulate the winning Horse;
The Coin that lost the Test Match; the huge Fist
Of the sub-human Champion-Pugilist;
The simpering Siren in the Bart.'s Divorce;
The well-connected Poisoner, tensely tried;
And the world-famed Bassoonist who has died.

Finally, O best and worst of rumour-breeders,
I damn your Circulation as a whole,
And leave you to your twice-ten-million readers
With deep condolence from my lenient soul.

The Grand Hotel

Superbly situated on a Lake
World-famed beyond the costliest Prima Donna
Who ever gargled a Puccini shake,—
The Grand Hotel (superimposed upon a
Villa evolved in vanished centuries
And denizened, long since, by real grandees)
While publishing on poster and prospectus

[134]

Its quite unique attractions which await us,
Refrains from offering to resurrect us
To an austere degree of social status.

Resolved to satirize Hotels-de-Luxe,
Shyly I sift the noodles from the crooks
Beneath whose bristly craniums a cigar
Juts and transmutes crude affluence to ash.
The Grand Hotel asks nothing but their cash;
The Grand Hotel contains a cock-tail bar
Where they can demonstrate by their behaviour
Hotel-de-Luxe aloofness from their Saviour.
   (The English visitors have motored off
   Into the mountains for a game of golf.)

The band concedes them Tosca with their tea.
Bored and expensive babble clogs the air.
Between two smooth white columns I can see
Gold and vermilion tulips. . . . Ambushed there
I criticize the ambulant outer-covers
That, costume-conscious, enter and withdraw
And in them all my satirist-self discovers
Prosperity that lives below the law. . . .
   (You ask what law I mean. . . . Well, my impression
   Is that these folk are poisoned by possession.)

Breach of Decorum

I have seen a man at Lady Lucre's table
Who stuck to serious subjects; spoke of Art
As if he were in earnest and unable

[135]

To ascertain its function in the smart
World where it shares a recreational part
With Bridge, best-selling Fiction, and the Stable.

I have heard that man (so destitute of nous
That he'd neglected even to be 'well-known;'
'*Whatever made her ask him to her house?*')
Talking to Lady Lucre in a tone
Of keen conviction that her social passion,
Purged of the volatilities of fashion,
Toiled after truth and spiritual perfection
Without regard for costume or complexion.

I have seen her fail, with petulant replies,
To localize him in his social senses:
I have observed her evening-party eyes
Evicted from their savoir-faire defences.
And while his intellectual gloom encroached
Upon the scintillance of champagne chatter,
In impotent embarrassment she broached
Golf, Goodwood Races, and the Cowes Regatta.

The luncheon over, Lady Lucre's set
Lolled on her lawn and lacked an epithet
Sufficiently severe for such a creature. . . .
'*Such dreadful taste!*' '*A positive blasphemer!*'
'*He actually referred to our Redeemer
As the world's greatest Socialistic teacher!*'

The Case for the Miners

Something goes wrong with my synthetic brain
When I defend the Strikers and explain
My reasons for not blackguarding the Miners.
'*What do you know?*' exclaim my fellow-diners
(Peeling their plovers' eggs or lifting glasses
Of mellowed *Château Rentier* from the table),
'*What do you know about the working classes?*'

I strive to hold my own; but I'm unable
To state the case succinctly. Indistinctly
I mumble about World-Emancipation,
Standards of Living, Nationalization
Of Industry; until they get me tangled
In superficial details; goad me on
To unconvincing vagueness. When we've wrangled
From soup to savoury, my temper's gone.

'*Why should a miner earn six pounds a week?*
Leisure! They'd only spend it in a bar!
Standard of life! You'll never teach them Greek,
Or make them more contented than they are!'
That's how my port-flushed friends discuss the Strike.
And that's the reason why I shout and splutter.
And that's the reason why I'd almost like
To see them hawking matches in the gutter.

[137]

The Blues at Lord's

Near-neighboured by a blandly boisterous Dean
Who 'hasn't missed the Match since '92,'
Proposing to perpetuate the scene
I concentrate my eyesight on the cricket.
The game proceeds, as it is bound to do
Till tea-time or the fall of the next wicket.

Agreeable sunshine fosters greensward greener
Than College lawns in June. Tradition-true,
The stalwart teams, capped with contrasted blue,
Exert their skill; adorning the arena
With modest, manly, muscular demeanour,—
Reviving memories in ex-athletes who
Are superannuated from agility,—
And (while the five-ounce fetish they pursue)
Admired by gloved and virginal gentility.

My intellectual feet approach this function
With tolerance and Public-School compunction;
Aware that, whichsoever side bats best,
Their partisans are equally well-dressed.
For, though the Government has gone vermilion
And, as a whole, is weak in Greek and Latin,
The fogies harboured by the august Pavilion
Sit strangely similar to those who sat in
That edifice when first the Dean went pious,—
For possible preferment sacrificed
His hedonistic and patrician bias,
And offered his complacency to Christ.

Meanwhile some Cantab slogs a fast half-volley
Against the ropes. 'Good shot, sir! O good shot!'
Ejaculates the Dean in accents jolly . . .
Will Oxford win? Perhaps. Perhaps they'll not.
Can Cambridge lose? Who knows? One fact seems sure;
That, while the Church approves, Lord's will endure.

Reynardism Revisited

A colour-print for Christmas. . . . Up the rise
Of rich green pasture move quick-clustering hounds
And red-coat riders. Crocus-yellow dyes
A patch of sunset laced by leafless trees.
One wavering tootle from the huntsman sounds
A mort for 'most unsatisfactory sport.'
And draws the pack's last straggling absentees
Out of the glooming purple of the covert.
Sad trails the cadent peeweep of a plover
Above the dim wet meadows by the brook,
While evening founders with a glowering look.
Clip-clop; along the glistening-puddled lane
The kennelward hoofs retreat. Night falls with rain.

.   .   .   .

Refortified by exercise and air,
I, jogging home astride my chestnut mare,
Grow half-humane, and question the propriety
Of *Foxes Torn to Bits in Smart Society*.

Spurts past me Fernie-Goldflake in his car . . .
I wonder if these Nimrods really are

[139]

Crassly unconscious that their Reynardism
Is (dare I say it?) an anachronism.
Can they rebut my heterodox defiance
Of *Hoick and Holloa as a Social Science?*
Or do they inwardly prognosticate
The Last (blank) Day; green shires degenerate
With unmolested poultry; drag-hound packs
Racing a bloodless aniseed aroma,
While cockney Gilpins gallop in their tracks;
And British Foxes, mythical as Homer,
Centuries-extinct, their odysseys forgotten.

My friends the Fernie-Goldflakes think me mad.
'*Extinct! The idea's preposterous! It's rotten
With every sort of Socialistic fad!*'

Shelley was called 'an atheistic worm'
By Goldflake's grandpapa . . .
                            Stands Shelley firm?

Sporting Acquaintances

I watched old squatting Chimpanzee: he traced
His painful patterns in the dirt: I saw
Red-haired Ourang-Utang, whimsical-faced,
Chewing a sportsman's meditative straw.
I'd known them years ago, and half-forgotten
They'd come to grief. (But how, I'd never heard,
Poor beggars!) Still, it seemed so rude and rotten
To stand and gape at them with never a word.

I ventured 'Ages since we met,' and tried
My candid smile of friendship. No success.
One scratched his hairy thigh, while t'other sighed
And glanced away. I saw they liked me less
Than when, on Epsom Downs, in cloudless weather,
We backed The Tetrarch and got drunk together.

Observations in Hyde Park

July proceeds. In ante-prandial strollings
I note the Season's climax. Cabbage-green,
Lush from humidity of cloud cajolings,
Predominates the vegetative scene.
Soaked, too, with blandishments of golden glare
(For, after all, the sun's a millionaire
Supremacied from super-tax), Hyde Park
Inhales its sunset swarms of biped forms
Prosperously promenading toward the dark.

But who are these that round the central road
Patrol superb in yellow-wheeled barouches?
What social magic keeps each carriage-load
Exempt from Lenin's Communistic Douches?
Observe the intrepid bonnets, how they flout
(From all that constitutes correct turn-out)
Darwin (who dared suggest arboreal monkey
As ancestor of all, from Queen to flunkey).

Meanwhile the scarlet band begins to render
A *Mendelssohn Selection*; and the throng

Of vesperal perisaunterers, touched by tender
Drum-bourdoned brass, discards stop-press for song.
The crested carriage halts; gem-dangled ears
Hearken in pensive frumpdom to the chords
That thrilled flounced-muslin maidenhood to tears;
The horses snort; she sighs for vanished lords.

Down Rotten Row the riders canter slow,
Keeping the old equestrian game alive.
Along warm asphalt paths foot-farers flow,
Pausing to watch pink pelargoniums thrive.
Pink pelargoniums thrive. Demure Democracy
Respects that commonwealth of sward-set bloom;
And no one signals the cockaded groom
To pluck bouquets for obsolete Aristocracy.

Storm on Fifth Avenue

A sallow waiter brings me six huge oysters . . .
Gloom shutters up the sunset with a plague
Of unpropitious twilight jagged asunder
By flashlight demonstrations. *Gee, what a peach
Of a climate!* (Pardon slang: these sultry storms
Afflict me with neurosis: rumbling thunder
Shakes my belief in academic forms.)

An oyster-coloured atmospheric rumpus
Beats up to blot the sunken daylight's gildings.
Against the looming cloud-bank, ivory-pale,
Stand twenty-storied blocks of office-buildings.
Snatched upward on a gust, lost news-sheets sail
Forlorn in lone arena of mid-air;

[142]

Flapping like melancholy kites, they scare
My gaze, a note of wildness in the scene.

Out on the pattering side-walk, people hurry
For shelter, while the tempest swoops to scurry
Across to Brooklyn. Bellying figures clutch
At wide-brimmed hats and bend to meet the weather,
Alarmed for fresh-worn silks and flurried feather.
Then hissing deluge splashes down to beat
The darkly glistening flatness of the street.
Only the cars nose on through rain-lashed twilight:
Only the Sherman Statue, angel-guided,
Maintains its mock-heroic martial gesture.

A sallow waiter brings me beans and pork . . .
Outside there's fury in the firmament.
Ice-cream, of course, will follow; and I'm content.
O Babylon! O Carthage! O New York!

Villa d'Este Gardens

'Of course you saw the Villa d'Este Gardens,'
Writes one of my Italianistic friends.
Of course; of course; I saw them in October,
Spired with pinaceous ornamental gloom
Of that arboreal elegy the cypress.

Those fountains, too, 'like ghosts of cypresses';—
(The phrase occurred to me while I was leaning
On an old balustrade; imbibing sunset;
Wrapped in my verse vocation)—how they linked me

With Byron, Landor, Liszt, and Robert Browning! . . .
A *Liebestraum* of Liszt cajoled my senses.

My language favoured Landor, chaste and formal.
My intellect (though slightly in abeyance)
Functioned against a Byronistic background.
Then Browning jogged my elbow; bade me hob-nob
With some forgotten painter of dim frescoes
That haunt the Villa's intramural twilight.

While roaming in the Villa d'Este Gardens
I felt like that . . . and fumbled for my note-book.

Fantasia on a Wittelsbach Atmosphere

Drab drugget paths protect these polished floors
From tourist-soled attrition. Guide-book phrases
Co-ordinate fatigued and baffled brains
With mute ex-regal affluence. Simpering faces
Exposed in state-saloons and corridors
Survive the modes of soporific reigns.

A baton, and a battle (was it Blenheim?)
Respectfully remote; the steed curvetting
Beneath his flushed Elector: what's the betting
He failed? . . . No gouty poet lives to pen him
Campaign-concluding odes. Mark, too, the mien
(Obese in ermine, sceptred and serene),
Of goggling Max Augustus! Where's the Court

That equerried his jinks down aisles of green
To chevy stags in sycophantic sport?

Nevertheless, while strolling past such glories
(Van Dyck to Winterhalter; stiff brocade
And powder, to frock-coats and whiskered smiles),
My spirit shares with monarchismal Tories
The fairy-tale of Flunkeydom, displayed
In feudal relicry of centuried styles.

   My sympathy for Soviets notwithstanding—
(Dare one deplore the dullness of Democracy?)
I am touched, I am enticed, by super-lavish
Expense; half-cultured coxcomb Kings commanding
In palacefuls the trappings of Autocracy,
With all their country's coffers ripe to ravish.

Outside, sham Renaissance facades evade
Modernity; a melancholic air
Half-masks them, while the sun-warmed windows stare
Affronted on the purposeless parade
Of pygmy visitors. In postures glum,
Like exiled Counts the statues mope aloof.
No vultured banner flaps above the roof:
And loyal gardens, drowsing in the hum
And slant of lapsing afternoon, seem sad.

   Fountains upheave pale plumes against the sky,
Murmuring, *Their Majesties came sauntering by—*
Was it but yesterday? . . . Proud fountains sigh
Toward the long glades in golden foliage clad,
Kurfürsts could do no wrong. . . . And the woods reply,
Take them for what they were, they weren't so bad!

Memorandum

Entering the strawberry-foliate demesne,
I pause (a tourist in the present tense),
Spectator of an architectural scene
Of Doric and Corinthian opulence.

Set to the musings of an autumn day
Serenely skied with undistracted grey,
Ducal redundancy (all balustrades,
Pilasters, porticoes, and colonnades)
Confronts me. (Vanbrugh made it for the man
Who carved rococo conquests for Queen Anne.)

In wars which burst before the South Sea Bubble
Muskets explode, hussars and pike-men plunder,
While Churchill, stimulating martial trouble,
Perturbs Palatinates with smoke and thunder.
Events unfold. The George Quartet contrives
William, Victoria, Edward; and at last
George Windsor's ermined; ruled by whom, arrives
Myself, obscurely pondering on the past—
Sententious thus . . . 'From halted History comes
The gusty bugling of Malbroukian fame;
And what was once imperious in a name
Recedes with desolate drub of death-led drums.

On regimental flags his fights persist;
But I've no zeal to bolster up the story
Of an imperiwigged stingy strategist
Who caracoled upon extortionate glory . . .'

Meanwhile the sun reburnishes the vanes
And orbs of Blenheim Palace; and the clock
Clangs out a modern hour, as if to mock
The mustiness of Marlborough's campaigns.

A Stately Exterior

The tenant absent (Scutcheon Hall is let
To Transatlantic opulence by a lord
Whose peerage pedigree adorns Debrett
With ancestries armorial and historic),
Discreetly I arrive to pace the sward
And ruminate, in unperturbed accord,
With mind appropriately metaphoric.

First let me praise the augustly planned approach
Whose vista, narrowing from wide walls of yew,
Needs nothing but a Queen Anne Period coach
(Plus absence of humanities like dew)
To give the prospect semblance of a print
In elegant autumnal aquatint.
Next let my gaze communicate its paean
Brainward and glorify the Jacobean
Rose-brickwork backed by dense arboreal green,—
The faded pink facade, that nectarine
Of pre-taxation Rent-roll style-stability
Planned for an impermutable nobility.

So far, so good. But wherefore its existence
In these dispalaced days? What mortals dare

House their domestic problems in so fair
A setting? . . . Silence . . . Then from foliaged distance
Some Tennysonian ring-dove calmly coos;
A gardener clicks quick shears beyond the yews;
Red Admirals and Painted Ladies bask
And float along the dahlia-brightened border;
Sunshine performs its horticultural task;
And ripened figs harbour the wasp-marauder.

An Old-World Effect

While blue-eyed children, goggle-faced and giggling,
Stare, swollen-cheeked (bad-mannered little wretches),
Two Nature-loving ladies dip their brushes,
Glance up, gaze down; with touches broad or niggling,
Remain absorbed in half-completed sketches
Where embryonic apple-blossom flushes
Round a decrepit cottage whence they catch
The ultimate rusticity of thatch.

You ask me why these artists have selected
An unhygienic dwelling as their theme . . .
'Have they no palate for the unexpected,—
No easel for the Cubist housing-scheme?'

A sapless unprolific Past they paint,
Who ramble through the guide-book toward the Quaint.
Meanwhile a blackbird pipes from the vicinity
His free fantasia against virginity.

In The National Gallery

Faces irresolute and unperplexed,—
Unspeculative faces, bored and weak,
Cruise past each patient victory of technique
Dimly desiring to enjoy the next
Yet never finding what they seem to seek.

Here blooms, recedes, and glows before their eyes
A quintessential world preserved in paint,
Calm vistas of long-vanished Paradise,
And ripe remembrances of sage and saint;
The immortality of changeless skies,
And all bright legendries of Time's creation . . .
    Yet I observe no gestures of surprise
    From those who straggle in to patronize
    The Art Collection of the English Nation.

The London Museum

Antiquarians, filling their noses
With the aromatic dust of some episode in History;
How I pity them their aversion from the flowing vistas of
    the Future!
For they organize an epoch as if it were a hall for obsolete
    utensils;
And the blunt broad sword must be catalogued according
    to its postulated Period.

But to me that am no antiquary, and a most indifferent
    historiographer,

This Museum is a mortuary for departed passions:
And I'd barter all the brocaded farthingales in
      Conservation
For a single scolding word from great Eliza's lips.

In holograph documents of the Commonwealth
Are memories and ghosts from yellow-candled councils;
Yet what are these, and even the death-mask of the
      Protector,
Compared with the gruff murmur that came to some
      nodding secretary,
When in politic debate the voices of Cromwell and
      Milton mingled?

I have learnt this afternoon, from a case of headless
      costumes,
That the Queen, when she bustled into the Great
      Exhibition,
Was wearing a sprigged silk dress and a bonnet with
      ostrich feathers.
From these we may deduce the inches of a once-imperial
      waist-line:
But who shall recover those heart-beats of *Victoria*, *Regina
      et Imperatrix*,
When she sailed into her Crystal Palace on the climacteric
      of a European culture?

It is four o'clock; and the London Museum is closing.
Outside, in the courtyard, a group of patriots lingers
To watch the young Heir to the Throne step into his
      hushed Rolls-Royce.
And I wonder, are they wiser than the Antiquarians?

In the Turner Rooms

(AT THE TATE GALLERY)

Into warm regions of Romance I stared:
Sat down; produced my note-book, and prepared
To fabricate iambics: something rich,
Serene, perpetual; tuned to concert-pitch:
Carthage without the climax; autumn-gold;
Red sunrise on a crag-set-castle . . . Bold
With pursuance of the encharioted Sublime,
I set my brains to work till closing-time.

Words failed me. Dido's harbour was a gleam
That vanished in white vapours: and the Garden
Of the Hesperides was but a dream
Shut in by storm-clad summits. On my toes
A mild enthusiast trod; and begged my pardon.
I bit my pencil; blinked; and blew my nose.

In canvases like these one ought to find
Imaginative moments; yet my mind
Jibs from their glory. Mellow rhymes with yellow;
And Turner was a wonder-working fellow:
But he forbids creation; fails to start
Co-ordinated memories . . . Now my heart
Leaps toward Romance and knows it, standing there
In that calm student with the red-brown hair,
Copying *The Death of Chatterton* with care
And missing all the magic. That young head
Is life, the unending challenge . . . Turner's dead.

On Some Portraits by Sargent

The Royal Academy has been much maligned
By modern æsthetes. . . . For myself, I find
More motives to applaud than to condemn
An edifice so apposite . . . ahem! . . .
Climbing the stairway in a cloud of chatter,
I am pledged to practise cogitant concision
And to reject all parenthetic matter
While ambulating round the Exhibition.

At this deaf-mute Reception where the Great
(With snobs whose wealth could wheedle them their
    places)
Survive in envied Sargentry (a state
No more achievable by mundane faces),
    Putting aside enigmas of technique,—
In calm cynosural canvases I seek
Some psycho-coefficient unconfessed . . .
A glum (though lingually-exempted) guest,
I analyse the output; which includes
Complacent persons opulently poised
In unawareness that their names are noised
In highbrow cliques as 'psychologic nudes'.

If Sargent could have called his soul his own
And had not been the hireling of the Rich,
There'd not be many portraits now re-shown
Of ladies lovelified to ball-room pitch;
Nor would these multiplied admirers crush
To crane their necks at sempiternal hostesses

Whom by the brilliant boredom of his brush
He silenced into fashion-dated ghostesses . . .
    Nor would my soul feel quite so mocked and chilly
    When I rejoin plebeian Piccadilly.

Evensong in Westminster Abbey

Out of the pattering flame-reflective street
Into the Abbey move my adagio feet,
Out of the lofty lamp-lit London dusk
Ferrying through vaulted sanctuaries a head
Calm, vesper-tolling, and subdued to shed
Gross thoughts and sabbatize the intemperate husk.

Gazing around, I glimpse the illustrious Dead:
Assembled ancestries of England loom.
Here, on this *Second Sunday after Epiphany*,
Milton and *Purcell* triumph from the tomb;
Spirits aspire on solemn-tongued antiphony,
And from their urns immortal garlands bloom.

Poets, musicians, orators, and Abstractions
Sponsorial, guard the suppliant congregation.
Fame with mum trumpet, posturing ripe attractions,
Sustains her simpering Eighteenth-Century station;
While *Shakespeare*, shy 'mid History's checked polemic,
Muses incognizant of his translation
Into a lingual culture-epidemic.
Charles Wesley; Isaac Watts; each now enjoys
Hymnistic perpetuity from boys

[153]

Chanting like scarlet-cassocked seraphim:
Here saintly *Keble* waits his Evening Hymn,
And hearkens, quiet, confident and humble.

John Gay looks glum . . . A clergyman ascends
The pulpit steps; smooths with one hand his hair,
And with the other hand begins to fumble
At manuscript of sermon. We prepare
Patience to listen. But *Disraeli* bends
Forward a little with his sceptic stare.
Time homilizes on. Grave ghosts are gone.
Diction has turned their monuments to stone:
Dogma has sent Antiquity to sleep
With sacrosanct stultiloquential drone.
But cryptical convulsions of the Past
Pervade the benediction's truce and sweep
Out on the organ's fugue-triumphal tone
When hosannatic Handel liberates us at last.

First Night: Richard III

Assassin with the murder-musing smile,
The horrible hunch-back, slim, and garbed in guile
And bulgy-dingy metal, seeks and wins
Unmasked soliloquies, superbly staged.
Slow fades each historied scene; but each begins
In similar pomp. He stabs King Henry caged,
(And wears a scarlet cloak). Next, gets engaged,
Vermilion-clad, black-legged, and sallow with sins.

Another King goes sick. He sneers (in brown).
The King dies, off. Astride his calm white steed
He broods and plots and lours on London town,
And gives two piping nephews all they need.
Then (crafty in a crimson velvet gown)
Limps towards the golden madness of a crown.

No single blood-stained sonnet could have shown
Richard, nor all his registrations told.
Now, shrunk and sable on his tragic throne,
He glowers envenomed (draped in cloth of gold).
. . . Big business with a candle . . . and his Queen
Beautifully poisoned somewhere in the wings
Then doom and gilded armour; and a scene
Of ghosts; dim, husky-voiced Shakespearian things.

.   .   .   .

The casualties were numerous: and at last
He died (in clashing brass-ware), tired but tense;
Lord of his own undoing, crazed, aghast,
And propertied regardless of expense.
And the whole proud production paled and passed,
Self-conscious, like its brilliant audience.

New York, March 1920.

A Post-Elizabethan Tragedy

'Tis a pity She's a Whore; last acted—Lord
Knows when! Revived (and played to-night before 'em)
By the Phœnician Stage Association;

Whose staunch subscribers, eager to applaud
Examples of archaic indecorum,
Combine with this their chaste discrimination.

Though Lamb extolled it, highbrows here allude
(Rapt in a Freudian future) to its 'crude
And obsolete psychology' . . . Detractors
Shatter my estimates. I'm disposed to think
(Wandering between the Acts in search of drink)
That the Audience gets between me and the Actors.

They squeeze and smoke; a jabbering, conscious crowd
Of intellectual fogies, fools, and freaks,—
A cultural inferno, parrot-loud
With clichés of accumulated weeks:
While, here and there, some calmly chatting Sage
(Immortalized by *Max*) exhibits fame
That awes the advertisers of our Age,—
Those Press-concerned celebrities who came
Intent to shine conspicuous in the stalls.

'Tis Pity She's a Whore . . . The curtain falls
On a composed but corpse-encumbered stage
Of expiated incest. Curtain-calls
Re-animate the agonists of passion.
And I'm aware, half-hostile and confused,
That, much though the Phœnicians were amused,
Old *Mermaid Dramatists* are out of fashion.

A Musical Critic Anticipates Eternity

If Someone, Something, somehow (as Man dreams)—
Some architectonic spirit-strength omniscient,—
Has wrought the clouded stars and all that seems
World, Universe, and Life (poor, blind, deficient)—
   If this be thus, and Music thrills the spheres,
   And I go thither when my feet have trod
   Past Death,—what chords might ecstasize my ears!
   What oratorios of Almighty God! . . .

Yet, seeing that all goes not too well on earth
In this harmonic venture known as Time,
I'm not too optimistic of the worth
Of problematic symphonies sublime:
   And, though I listen aureoled and meek
   To compositions by the Holy Trinity,
   Who knows but I may write (in my critique)—
   'The music was devoid of all divinity!'

Hommage à Mendelssohn

Play me the languishing *Prelude in A flat;*
And muse, while sentiment pervades the strings,
Of Love's macassar-oiled Magnificat
Wafting the world on Mendelssohnian wings.
   Scorn not mild mid-Victorian hearts unloaded
   Of universal yearnings; thus they sighed . . .
   Think, too, how we ourselves may be outmoded,—
   Shorn of our psycho-analytic pride.

[157]

Those sinking chords can charm us and assuage
With amiable concinnity of style;
So let us welcome them for what they're worth.
(Still gazing steadfast toward that epic age
When boudoir beauty shall no more beguile
And sentiment is elbowed off the earth.)

Concert-Interpretation

(LE SACRE DU PRINTEMPS)

The audience pricks an intellectual Ear . . .
Stravinsky . . . *Quite the Concert of the Year!*

Forgetting now that none-so-distant date
When they (or folk facsimilar in state
Of mind) first heard with hisses—hoots—guffaws—
This abstract Symphony (they booed because
Stravinsky jumped their Wagner palisade
With modes that seemed cacophonous and queer),
Forgetting now the hullabaloo they made,
The Audience pricks an intellectual ear.

Bassoons begin . . . Sonority envelops
Our auditory innocence; and brings
To Me, I must admit, some drift of things
Omnific, seminal, and adolescent.
Polyphony through dissonance develops
A serpent-conscious Eden, crude but pleasant;
While vibro-atmospheric copulations
With mezzo-forte mysteries of noise

Prelude Stravinsky's statement of the joys
That unify the monkeydom of nations.

This matter is most indelicate indeed!
Yet one perceives no symptom of stampede.
The Stalls remain unruffled: craniums gleam:
Swept by a storm of pizzicato chords,
Elaborate ladies re-assure their lords
With lifting brows that signify 'Supreme!'
While orchestrated gallantry of goats
Impugns the astigmatic programme-notes.

In the Grand Circle one observes no sign
Of riot: peace prevails along the line.
And in the Gallery, cargoed to capacity,
No tremor bodes eruptions and alarms.
They are listening to this not-quite-new audacity
As though it were by someone dead,—like Brahms.

But savagery pervades Me; I am frantic
With corybantic rupturing of laws.
Come, dance, and seize this clamorous chance to function
Creatively,—abandoning compunction
In anti-social rhapsodic applause!
Lynch the conductor! Jugulate the drums!
Butcher the brass! Ensanguinate the strings!
Throttle the flutes! . . . Stravinsky's April comes
With pitiless pomp and pain of sacred springs . . .
Incendiarize the Hall with resinous fires
Of sacrificial fiddles scorched and snapping! . . .

Meanwhile the music blazes and expires;
And the delighted Audience is clapping.

[159]

Founder's Feast

Old as a toothless Regius Professor
Ebbed the Madeira wine. Loquacious graduates
Sipped it with sublimation. They'd been drinking
The health of . . . was it Edward the Confessor?
A solemn banquet glowed in every cheek,
While nicotinean fumes befogged the roof
And the carved gallery where prim choristers
Sang like Pre-Raphaelite angels through the reek.

Gowns, rose and scarlet in flamingo ranks,
Adorned the dais that shone with ancient silver;
And guests of honour gazed far down the Hall
With precognition of returning thanks.
There beamed the urbanest Law-lord on the Bench,
Debating with the Provost (ceremonious
In flushed degrees of vintage scholarship),
The politics of Plato,—and the French.

But on the Provost's left, in gold and blue,
Sat . . . O my God! . . . great Major-General Bluff . . .
Enough enough enough enough enough!

Sheldonian Soliloquy

(DURING BACH'S B MINOR MASS)

My music-loving Self this afternoon
(Clothed in the gilded surname of Sassoon)
Squats in the packed Sheldonian and observes

An intellectual bee-hive perched and seated
In achromatic and expectant curves
Of buzzing, sunbeam-flecked, and overheated
Accommodation. Skins perspire . . . But hark! . . .
Begins the great *B minor Mass* of Bach.

The choir sings *Gloria in excelsis Deo*
With confident and well-conducted *brio*.
Outside, a motor-bike makes impious clatter,
Impinging on our Eighteenth-Century trammels.
God's periwigged : He takes a pinch of snuff.
The music's half-rococo. . . . Does it matter
While those intense musicians shout the stuff
In Catholic Latin to the cultured mammals
Who agitate the pages of their scores ? . . .

Meanwhile, in Oxford sunshine out of doors,
Birds in collegiate gardens rhapsodize
Antediluvian airs of worm-thanksgiving.
To them the austere and buried Bach replies
With song that from ecclesiasmus cries
Eternal *Resurrexit* to the living.

Hosanna in excelsis chants the choir
In pious contrapuntal jubilee.
Hosanna shrill the birds in sunset fire.
And Benedictus sings my heart to Me.

Early Chronology

Slowly the daylight left our listening faces.

Professor Brown with level baritone
Discoursed into the dusk.
                                        Five thousand years
He guided us through scientific spaces
Of excavated History; till his lone
Roads of research grew blurred; and in our ears
Time was the rumoured tongues of vanished races,
And Thought a chartless Age of Ice and Stone.

The story ended: and the darkened air
Flowered while he lit his pipe; an aureole glowed
Enwreathed with smoke: the moment's match-light
        showed
His rosy face, broad brow, and smooth grey hair,
Backed by the crowded book-shelves.
                                        In his wake
An archæologist began to make
Assumptions about aqueducts (he quoted
Professor Sandstorm's book); and soon they floated
Through desiccated forests; mangled myths;
And argued easily round megaliths.

Beyond the college garden something glinted;
A copper moon climbed clear above black trees.
Some Lydian coin? . . . Professor Brown agrees
That copper coins *were* in that Culture minted.
But, as her whitening way aloft she took,
I thought she had a pre-dynastic look.

Solar Eclipse

Observe these blue solemnities of sky
Offering for the academes of after-ages
A mythologic welkin freaked with white!
   Listen: one tiny tinkling rivulet
Accentuates the super-sultry stillness
That drones on ripening landscapes which imply
Serene Parnassus plagued with amorous goats.

Far down the vale Apollo has pursued
The noon-bedazzled nymph whose hunted heart
Holds but the trampling panic whence it fled.
And now the heavens are piled with darkening trouble
And counter-march of clouds that troop intent
Fire-crested into conflict.
                    Daphne turns
At the wood's edge in bronze and olive gloom:
Sickness assails the sun, whose blazing disc
Dwindles: the Eden of those auburn slopes
Lours in the tarnished copper of eclipse.

Yet virgin, in her god-impelled approach
To Græco-Roman ravishment, she waits
While the unsated python slides to crush
Her lust-eluding fleetness. Envious Jove
Rumbles Olympus. All the classic world
Leans breathless toward the legend she creates.

From thunderous vapour smites the immortal beam . . .
Then, crowned with fangs of foliage, flames the god.

Apollo! . . . Up the autumn valley echoes
A hollow shout from nowhere. Daphne's limbs
Lapse into laureldom: green-shadowed flesh
Writhes arborescent: glamour obscures her gaze
With blind and bossed distortion. She escapes.

The Utopian Times

Old Caspar (that's myself) all doings done,
Sits at his creeper-covered cottage door,
Warmed by the rural radiance of the sun.

He watches for the postman to appear,
Knowing that he brings the 'newspaper' once more,
And thanks him when he comes. For the austere
Utopian Times arrives but once a year,
(Published on Shakespeare's Birthday) and is, indeed,
The last surviving 'newspaper' men read
On our contented island, once the core
Of an inconvenient 'Empire,' now 'no more.'

Old Caspar's cheerful. *The Utopian Times*
Announces that 'no credible report
Has reached us, in twelve months, of any 'crimes'
Of the once-prevalent, punishable sort.
The antiquated labyrinths of the Law
Have now become entirely obsolete.
Quite lately, for its final 'Session,' we saw
The last of the old 'Courts of Justice' meet.
A few 'financiers' plotted and acquired
Public opprobrium by their quaint adventure.

[164]

(They were condemned to spade-work, it transpired,
By the Vegetable Growers' Board of Censure.)'

Old Caspar's paper tells him that 'although
Passion for Literature pervades the Nation,
Books are infrequent. Authors wisely know
That Literature needs lengthy incubation.'
'Except for individual recreation,
Interest in ''Sport'' continues to decrease.'
'Scientists report a healthy population . . .
The Seventieth Anniversary of Peace.'
'Longevity is prevalent . . .' ('That's quite true,'
Thinks Caspar, who himself is a hundred and two.)

'Hum-drum,' he mutters; and turns the page to find
(Headed 'A Curious Relic of the Past')
A paragraph which 'takes him back,' in mind,
To the Imperfect Age which changed so fast.

' ''Lord'' Bags, who died last March, despised and old,
Had influence once. Employer of no less
Than fourteen hundred editors, he controlled
A vast proportion of ''the Public Press''.
His catchpenny career was quickly ended
By the ''Statute for Prevention of False News''.
In later life he stubbornly defended
His methods by asserting that ''the Jews
Were a World Menace''; adding that he had ''done
More for the World than almost anyone.'' '

Thus Caspar read, before he went to rest,
News from the 'Social State' where he was guest.
And if you doubt the ingredients of these rhymes,
Buy your own copy of *The Utopian Times*.

1924.

Mammoniac Ode

I

Hark, hark, the Mark in the Money Market sings!
And sweet Swiss francs in Bernese Banks
Yodel to Mammon a million thanks
For swift and profitable flight on funded wings.
To Mammon's face of many facets,
'Firm in tone' they raise their song;
'Fluctuant Bonds and Frozen Assets
Unto us no more belong.'

II

Toll for the brave
Gold Standard sunk below the European wave.
For Britain's Gold Redemption Policy suspended,
And the Parity of the Pound (Alas, poor Yorick!) ended,
Lament from fiscal throats,
O patriot Five-Pound Notes;
And let your dirge with Wage Reductions be well
    blended.

III

O Franco-franc, O Dollar, and O Florin,
Exceed your rights, ferocious-fanged and foreign!
Pengo, Peseta, and Colonial Pound,
Abjure your mineral ancestry, and be
More glorious than mere gold from underground;
Soar, sag; and move portentously unsound;
Cause all the trouble you can; but O—be free!

IV

Finally, O English Dictionary, this conundrum settle,
And aid me to be poet-laureate of the aureate . . .
'Non-rusting yellow malleable ductile metal
Of high specific gravity'; (*as good as gold*).
'Gold can be foil or dust or leaf; beaten or rolled.
Coins made of this. Money in specie. Bullion. Wealth.'
Gold this; gold that. Pure gold. Gold cannot buy good
health.
Gold plate. Resources. Interest. Incomes. Power of
purchase.
Pays Unemployment. Buys Champagne, and builds new
churches . . .
The finest Sport on earth is job-stock Speculation . . .
Deliver us, O Lord, from Currency Inflation.

September 30, 1931.

Memorial Service for an Honest Soldier

Memorial Service. Mid-day. The Police
Are there in Palace Yard to keep the peace
Among phlegmatic lookers-on. Half-mast,
The flag, heraldic-emblemed, flaps and bulges.
Watching this Abbey function, one indulges
A taste for public figures of the past.

An incorruptible persistent man
Who ended as Field-Marshal and began
As private soldier, in our thoughts to-day
Takes, when his mortal manliness is mute,
The Nation's last invisible salute,
And from Officialdom receives his pay.

'*Fight the good fight with all your might.*' they sing.
The Abbey looks its best; pale sunshine falls
Through glowing glass on monumental walls
And vainly carven virtues,—busts that bring
Null names to lifeless life. . . . Sunlight and sound
Seem to be streaming on their way together
Like Time idealized, as though they'd found
Some antidote for earth's contentious weather.

The congregation gets itself arranged,
With murmurous rustle, for the benediction.
Now for a miracle! Let hearts be changed
And truth emerge from fraudulence and fiction.

Now let the Cross of Christ convert the crook,
And self-convict the subtly scheming knave,

Make Mammon merciful, and from their grave
Raise up the unperjured spirits that forsook
Long since the blasphemous hearts they could not save.

The choir precedes, in listless prim procession,
The cross-bearer, exalting Faith; and then
The gold-coped Abbey clergy, whose profession
Has made them, outwardly, world-weary men.
Officials follow. Law in wig and gown,
Clean-shaved and circumspect. And the type
Of immemorial diplomat comes down
The centuries, elegant and over-ripe,
And representing France. Then, face by face,
Those persons, long familiar through the Press,
Who've governed Albion's muddles by some guess
Of God,—not always running the straight race.

Thus, with a formal and unfeeling show,
Contemporaneous life performs its part.
History records careers; and does not know
The secret memoirs of the human heart.
But while I watch prestige step slowly out
Like actors in a mediæval play
I can't repress ironic thoughts about
The 'representatives' who're here to-day.
The man they wear silk hats for has meanwhile
Entered his unmolestable immunity;
And can afford, as dead men do, to smile
Serenely at this G.H.Q. community.

1933.

The Traveller to His Soul

That problem which concerns me most—about
Which I have entertained the gravest doubt—
Is, bluntly stated, 'Have I got a soul?'
And, soulhood granted, while millenniums roll,
Will it inhabit some congenial clime,
Detached from thoughts indigenous to Time,—
Anonymous in what we name 'the Whole'?

'O Soul, consider what you are,' I say;
'How seldom you exert your white authority
On the bemused and sense-instructed way
In which your apparatus spends his day:
Regard the overwhelming mob-majority
Of mundane apprehensions which compose
One week-day of what Ego feels and knows.'

.   .   .   .

Souls have their Sunday morning, belled and bright;
And in the night they move in landless light.
(Skulls thus affirm their legend.) Souls arise
Through flames of martyrdom, absolved and wise,
And those who moved in gloom regain their sight.

'The starry heavens above me,' someone said,
'And the moral law within me, these are things
Which fill my mind with admiration.' . . . Head
And heart, thus prompted, feel aware of wings
And soaring Gothic-aisled imaginings . . .
Soul, will you feel like that when I am dead?

1933.

The Facts

Can a man face the facts of life and laugh? . . .
Swift faced them and died mad, deaf and diseased.
Shakespeare spoke out, went home, and wrote no more.
Oblivion was the only epitaph
They asked, as private persons, having eased
Their spirits of the burden that they bore.

The facts of life are fierce. One feels a wraith
When facing them with luminous lyric faith.
Daring to look within us, we discern
The jungle. To the jungle we return
More easily than most of us admit.
In this thought-riddled twentieth-century day
I cannot read—say 'Gulliver'—and feel gay,
Or share—in 'Lear'—the pleasure of the Pit.

1932.

THE HEART'S JOURNEY

I

Song, be my soul; set forth the fairest part
Of all that moved harmonious through my heart;
And gather me to your arms; for we must go
To childhood's garden when the moon is low
And over the leaf-shadow-latticed grass
The whispering wraiths of my dead selves repass.

Soul, be my song; return arrayed in white;
Lead home the loves that I have wronged and slain:
Bring back the summer dawns that banished night
With distant-warbling bird-notes after rain. . . .
Time's way-worn traveller I. And you, O song,
O soul, my Paradise laid waste so long.

II

Sing bravely in my heart, you patient birds
Who all this weary winter wait for spring;
Sing, till such wonder wakens in my words
As I have known long since, beyond all voicing,—
Strong with the beat of blood, wild on the wing,
Rebellious and rejoicing.

Watch with me, inward solemn influence,
Invisible, intangible, unkenned;

[175]

Wind of the darkness that shall bear me hence;
O life within my life, flame within flame,
Who mak'st me one with song that has no end,
And with that stillness whence my spirit came.

III

As I was walking in the gardens where
Spring touched the glooms with green, stole over me
A sense of wakening leaves that filled the air
With boding of Elysian days to be.

Cold was the music of the birds; and cold
The sunlight, shadowless with misty gold:
It seemed I stood with Youth on the calm verge
Of some annunciation that should bring
With flocks of silver angels, ultimate Spring
Whence all that life had longed for might emerge.

IV

What you are I cannot say;
Only this I know full well—
When I touched your face to-day
Drifts of blossom flushed and fell.

Whence you came I cannot tell;
Only—with your joy you start
Chime on chime from bell on bell
In the cloisters of my heart.

V

While I seek you, far away,
(Yesterday, yesterday,)
Wakeful since we laughed and parted,
How can I recover
Joy that made Elysian-hearted,
Loved and lover?

Can my night-long thoughts regain
Time-locked loveliness and laughter?
Can your presence in my brain
Be rebuilt such æons after?
Can it be so far away—
Yesterday, yesterday?

VI

Now when we two have been apart so long
And you draw near, I make you mine in song.
Waiting you in my thought's high lonely tower
That looks on starlit hushed Elysian gloom,
I know your advent certain as the flower
Of daybreak that on breathless vales shall bloom.

Oh, never hasten now; for time's all sweet,
And you are clad in the garment of my dreams:
Led by my heart's enchanted cry, your feet
Move with the murmur of forest-wandering streams
Through earth's adoring darkness to discover
The Paradise of your imperfect lover.

VII

In me, past, present, future meet
To hold long chiding conference.
My lusts usurp the present tense
And strangle Reason in his seat.
My loves leap through the future's fence
To dance with dream-enfranchised feet.

In me the cave-man clasps the seer,
And garlanded Apollo goes
Chanting to Abraham's deaf ear.
In me the tiger sniffs the rose.
   Look in my heart, kind friends, and tremble,
   Since there your elements assemble.

VIII

Since thought is life, God's martyrdoms were good,
And saints are trumps, no matter what they did.
Therefore I celebrate Sebastian's blood,
And glory with Lorenzo on his grid,
And likewise with all victims, bruised by boulders,
Stabbed by sadistic swords, on pikes impaled,
Who propped their Paradise on bleeding shoulders
And bred tumultuous pomps when princes failed.

Thus for their murdered Master,—thus for his dreamed
Utopia,—from a crookèd Roman cross,
Heavenward on crimson clouds their conquest streamed
To touch His lips in life-redeeming loss.

[178]

IX

What is Stonehenge? It is the roofless past;
Man's ruinous myth; his uninterred adoring
Of the unknown in sunrise cold and red;
His quest of stars that arch his doomed exploring.

And what is Time but shadows that were cast
By these storm-sculptured stones while centuries fled?
The stones remain; their stillness can outlast
The skies of history hurrying overhead.

X

Farewell to a Room

Room, while I stand outside you in the gloom,
Your tranquil-toned interior, void of me,
Seems part of my own self which I can see. . . .

Light, while I stand outside you in the night,
Shutting the door on what has housed so much,
Nor hand, nor eye, nor intellect could touch,—
Cell, to whose firelit walls I say farewell,
Could I condense five winters in one thought,
Then might I know my unknown self and tell
What our confederate silences have wrought.

XI

'*When I'm alone*'—the words tripped off his tongue
As though to be alone were nothing strange.
'*When I was young*,' he said; '*when I was young. . . .*'

I thought of age, and loneliness, and change.
I thought how strange we grow when we're alone,
And how unlike the selves that meet, and talk,
And blow the candles out, and say good-night.
Alone . . . The word is life endured and known.
It is the stillness where our spirits walk
And all but inmost faith is overthrown.

XII

In the stars we have seen the strangeness of our state;
Wisdomless men, we have lifted up our eyes:
From the stars we have asked an augury of our fate,
And our speech has made them symbols of the wise.

O star that youth's awakening eyes have seen,
Sustain us in our nearness to the night:
And you, O storm-hid Hesperus, make serene
Our loss of this loved heritage of light.

XIII

Strangeness of Heart

When I have lost the power to feel the pang
Which first I felt in childhood when I woke
And heard the unheeding garden bird who sang
Strangeness of heart for me while morning broke;
Or when in latening twilight sure with spring,
Pausing on homeward paths along the wood,
No sadness thrills my thought while thrushes sing,
And I'm no more the listening child who stood
So many sunsets past and could not say
What wandering voices called from far away:
    When I have lost those simple spells that stirred
    My being with an untranslated song,
    Let me go home for ever; I shall have heard
    Death; I shall know that I have lived too long.

XIV

When Selfhood can discern no comfort for its cares,
Whither may I turn but to you whose strength my spirit
    shares?
Where may I find but in you,
Beethoven, Bach, Mozart,
Timeless, eternally true,
Heavens that may hold my heart?
Rivers of peace that run beyond the setting sun,
And where all names are one, green Paradise apart.

XV

Grandeur of Ghosts

When I have heard small talk about great men
I climb to bed; light my two candles; then
Consider what was said; and put aside
What Such-a-one remarked and Someone-else replied.

They have spoken lightly of my deathless friends,
(Lamps for my gloom, hands guiding where I stumble,)
Quoting, for shallow conversational ends,
What Shelley shrilled, what Blake once wildly
      muttered. . . .

How can they use such names and be not humble?
I have sat silent; angry at what they uttered.
The dead bequeathed them life; the dead have said
What these can only memorize and mumble.

XVI

Alone, I hear the wind about my walls . . .
Wind of the city night, south-west and warm,—
Rain-burdened wind, your homely sound recalls
Youth; and a distant country-side takes form,
Comforting with memory-sight my town-taxed brain . . .
Wind from familiar fields and star-tossed trees,
You send me walking lonely through dark and rain
Before I'd lost my earliest ecstasies.

Wind of the city-lamps, you speak of home
And how into this homelessness I've come
Where all's uncertain but my will for power
To ask of life no more than life can earn . . .
Wind from the past, you bring me the last flower
From gardens where I'll nevermore return.

XVII

To an Eighteenth Century Poet

Old friend (for such you have lately grown to be
Since your tranquillities have tuned with mine),
Sitting alone, your poems on my knee,
In hours of contemplative candleshine,
I sometimes think your ghost revisits me
And lives upon my lips from line to line.

Dead though you are, the quiet-toned persistence
Of what you tell me with your sober skill
Reminds me how terrestrial existence
Plays tricks with death, and, unextinguished still,
Turns home in loveliest hauntings from the distance
Of antiquated years and works its will.

This is the power, the privilege, the pride
And rich morality of those who write
That hearts may be their highway. They shall ride
Conquering uncharted countries with the bright
Rewards of what they wrought in living light . . .
Who then shall dare to say that they have died?

XVIII

To an Old Lady Dead

Old lady, when last year I sipped your tea
And wooed you with my deference to discuss
The elegance of your embroidery,
I felt no forethought of our meeting thus.
    Last week your age was 'almost eighty-three.'
    To-day you own the eternal over-plus.
    These moments are 'experience' for me;
    But not for you; not for a mutual 'us'.

I visit you unwelcomed; you've no time
Left to employ in afternoon politeness.
You've only Heaven's great stairway now to climb,
And your long load of years has changed to lightness.
    When Oxford belfries chime you do not hear,
    Nor in this mellow-toned autumnal brightness
    Observe an English-School-like atmosphere . . .
    You have inherited everlasting whiteness.

You lived your life in grove and garden shady
Of social Academe, good talk and taste:
But now you are a very quiet old lady,
Stiff, sacrosanct, and alabaster-faced.
    And, while I tip-toe awe-struck from your room,
    I fail to synthesize your earth-success
    With this, your semblance to a sculptured tomb
    That clasps a rosary of nothingness.

XIX

To One in Prison

To-day we have remembered sacrifice and glory
And the Cenotaph with flowers is overstocked:
A single gun to soundlessness has clocked
And unified King, Communist, and Tory. . . .
I have listened to your broken stumbling story,
And trespassed in your mind, slum-built and shoddy.
You too have shared the Silence; you have knelt
In the cheerless Prison chapel; you have felt
Armistice Day emotion brim your body.

Six years, you say, you've worked at baking bread
(A none-too-wholesome task that must be done
By those whom God appoints). You are twenty-one
(Though I'd have guessed you less). Your father's dead
(Run over by a lorry, I think you said,
In the Great War, while coming home on leave).
Your brother got in trouble and spent three years
In Borstal (all these facts I can believe
Without the reinforcement of your tears).

Your brother failed completely to 'make good';
Your brother died; committed suicide
By turning on the gas, a twelve-month since.
Now you're in prison for stealing what you could:
Mother's in prison for the same offence:
And I've no reason to suspect you lied
When you informed me that you 'only tried

[185]

To stick to mother.' I was touched. You stood
So young, so friendless, so remorseful-eyed.

Therefore I find myself compelled to add
A footnote on your candour and humility.
You seem to me a not insensitive lad
Of average emotional ability.
You've 'been upset to-day.' 'By what?' I query.
'By the two-minute silence.' Then your weeping . . .
And then your face, so woebegone and weary.
And now—what use, the pity that I am heaping
Upon your head? What use—to wish you well
And slam the door? Who knows? . . . My heart, not
      yours, can tell.

XX

To One Who was With Me in the War

It was too long ago—that Company which we served
      with . . .
We call it back in visual fragments, you and I,
Who seem, ourselves, like relics casually preserved with
Our mindfulness of old bombardments when the sky
With blundering din blinked cavernous.
                          Yet a sense of power
Invades us when, recapturing an ungodly hour
Of ante-zero crisis, in one thought we've met
To stand in some redoubt of Time,—to share again
All but the actual wetness of the flare-lit rain,
All but the living presences who haunt us yet
With gloom-patrolling eyes.

Remembering, we forget
Much that was monstrous, much that clogged our souls
      with clay
When hours were guides who led us by the longest way—
And when the worst had been endured could still disclose
Another worst to thwart us . . .
                    We forget our fear . . .
And, while the uncouth Event begins to lour less near,
Discern the mad magnificence whose storm-light throws
Wild shadows on these after-thoughts that send your
      brain
Back beyond Peace, exploring sunken ruinous roads.
Your brain, with files of flitting forms hump-backed with
      loads,
On its own helmet hears the tinkling drops of rain,—
Follows to an end some night-relief, and strangely sees
The quiet no-man's-land of daybreak, jagg'd with trees
That loom like giant Germans . . .
                    I'll go with you, then,
Since you must play this game of ghosts. At listening-posts
We'll peer across dim craters; joke with jaded men
Whose names we've long forgotten. (Stoop low there;
      it's the place
The sniper enfilades.) Round the next bay you'll meet
A drenched platoon-commander; chilled, he drums his
      feet
On squelching duck-boards; winds his wrist-watch; turns
      his head,
And shows you how you looked,—your ten-years-
      vanished face,
Hoping the War will end next week. . . .
                    What's that you said?

XXI

On Passing the New Menin Gate

Who will remember, passing through this Gate,
The unheroic Dead who fed the guns?
Who shall absolve the foulness of their fate,—
Those doomed, conscripted, unvictorious ones?
    Crudely renewed, the Salient holds its own.
    Paid are its dim defenders by this pomp;
    Paid, with a pile of peace-complacent stone,
    The armies who endured that sullen swamp.

Here was the world's worst wound. And here with pride
'Their name liveth for ever,' the Gateway claims.
Was ever an immolation so belied
As these intolerably nameless names?
Well might the Dead who struggled in the slime
Rise and deride this sepulchre of crime.

XXII

From a Fugue by Bach

Musing my way through a sombre and favourite fugue
By Bach who disburdens my soul but perplexes my fingers,
I heard, as it were in the past of my being that listened,
Echoes of antiphones chanted remotely: I visioned
Martyrs in Glory who stood upon clouds while the singers
Lifted their hearts into heaven, by music unprisoned.

If this in itself were enough, I am crowned with the best.
But the vision in silence has vanished: I know but my
    need
To be clearing my lofts of their lumber, to build with my
    breath
The litany leading me onward, the intimate creed
That must hold me enhumbled, barred out from abodes of
    the blest:
For my prayer must be laden with life and the patience
    that saith,
'In our bodies we bide, and the end of the body is death.'

Praying I know not to whom in this musicless room
Where my soul like the flame of a candle in ecstasy stood,
I gaze at my life in a mirror, desirous of good.
And my solitude girds me with ghosts, with invisible
    words:
In the mirror I see but the face that is me, that is mine;
And the notes of the fugue that were voices from vastness
    divine.

XXIII

At the Grave of Henry Vaughan

Above the voiceful windings of a river
An old green slab of simply graven stone
Shuns notice, overshadowed by a yew.
Here Vaughan lies dead, whose name flows on for ever
Through pastures of the spirit washed with dew
And starlit with eternities unknown.

Here sleeps the Silurist; the loved physician;
The face that left no portraiture behind;
The skull that housed white angels and had vision
Of daybreak through the gateways of the mind.
Here faith and mercy, wisdom and humility
(Whose influence shall prevail for evermore)
Shine. And this lowly grave tells Heaven's tranquillity.
And here stand I, a suppliant at the door.

XXIV

A Midnight Interior

To-night while I was pondering in my chair
I saw for the first time a circle of brightness
Made by my patient lamp up on the ceiling.
It shone like a strange flower; and then my stare
Discovered an arctic snowstorm in that whiteness;
And then some pastoral vale of rayed revealing.

White flowers were in a bowl beside my book;
In midnight's miracle of light they glowed,
And every petal there in silence showed
My life the way to wonder with a look.

O inwardness of trust,—intelligence,—
Release my soul through every door of sense:
Give me new sight; O grant me strength to find
From lamp and flower simplicity of mind.

XXV
One Who Watches

We are all near to death. But in my friends
I am forewarned too closely of that nearness.
Death haunts their days that are; in him descends
The darkness that shall change their living dearness
    To something different, made within my mind
    By memories and recordings and convenings
    Of voices heard through veils and faces blind
    To the kind light of my autumnal gleanings.

Not so much for myself I feel that fear
As for all those in whom my loves must die;
Thus, like some hooded death, I stand apart
And in their happiest moments I can hear
Silence unending, when those lives must lie
Hoarded like happy summers in my heart.

XXVI

It has been told and shall be told again
How Night and Day visit the souls of men;
How lissom fiends out of their lusts arise
Till hopeless hell emerges in their eyes;
And how in those dominions of despair
World-ravening ghosts make masques of gloom and glare.

[191]

But O, more strange,—and who shall say how strong?—
Those imageries of peace which men behold
Through inmost prayer in world-encircling white . . .
And who shall say to which we most belong,
In whom the incongruous elements unfold
Legions of darkness lost and found in light?

XXVII

I cannot pray with my head,
Nor aspire from bended knees;
But I saw in a dream the dead
Moving among green trees.
I saw the living green
Uprising from the rock.
This have I surely seen,
Though the morning mind may mock.

XXVIII

All-Souls' Day

Close-wrapped in living thought I stand
Where death and daybreak divide the land,—
Death and daybreak on either hand
For exit and for entry;
While shapes like wind-blown shadows pass,
Lost and lamenting, 'Alas, alas,

This body is only shrivelling grass,
And the soul a starlit sentry
Who guards, and as he comes and goes,
Points now to daybreak's burning rose,
And now toward worldhood's charnel close
Leans with regretless warning' . . .
   I hear them thus—O thus I hear
   My doomed companions crowding near,
   Until my faith, absolved from fear,
   Sings out into the morning,
   And tells them how we travel far,
   From life to life, from star to star;
   Exult, unknowing what we are;
   And quell the obscene derision
   Of demon-haunters in our heart
   Who work for worms and have no part
   In Thee, O ultimate power, who art
   Our victory and our vision.

XXIX

The Power and the Glory

Let there be life, said God. And what He wrought
Went past in myriad marching lives, and brought
This hour, this quiet room, and my small thought
Holding invisible vastness in its hands.

Let there be God, say I. And what I've done
Goes onward like the splendour of the sun
And rises up in rapture and is one
With the white power of conscience that commands.

Let life be God. . . . What wail of fiend or wraith
Dare mock my glorious angel where he stands
To fill my dark with fire, my heart with faith?

XXX

The wisdom of the world is this. To say, *There is*
No other wisdom but to gulp what time can give.
　　To guard no inward vision winged with mysteries;
　　To hear no voices haunt the hurrying hours we live;
　　To keep no faith with ghostly friends; never to know
　　Vigils of sorrow crowned when loveless passions
　　　　fade . . .
From wisdom such as this to find my gloom I go,
Companioned by those powers who keep me unafraid.

XXXI

Conclusion

An image dance of change
Throngs my dim-sighted flesh,
To music's air-built mesh
Move thoughts for ever strange.
I am so woven of sense
And subtlety uncharted
That I must vanish hence
Blind-souled and twilight-hearted.

[194]

Soon death the hooded lover
Shall touch my house of clay,
And life-lit eyes discover
That in the warbling grey
I have been early waking,
And while the dawn was breaking
Have stolen afield to find
That secrecy which quivers
Beyond the skies and rivers
And cities of the mind.

Till then, my thought shall strive
That living I may not lose
The wonder of being alive,
Nor time's least gift refuse.

For, though the end be night,
This wonder and this white
Astonishment of sight
Make hours of magic shine;
And heaven's a blaze and bloom
Of transience and divine
Inheritance of doom.

XXXII

A flower has opened in my heart . . .
What flower is this, what flower of spring,
What simple, secret thing?
It is the peace that shines apart,
The peace of daybreak skies that bring
Clear song and wild swift wing.

Heart's miracle of inward light,
What powers unknown have sown your seed
And your perfection freed? . . .
O flower within me wondrous white,
I know you only as my need
And my unsealèd sight.

XXXIII

A Last Judgment

He heard an angel say *now look for love*, and *look
For lust* the burning city of his heart replied.
And the angel, whom his heart had life-time-long denied,
In silence stood apart and watched him while he took
The scarlet and the sceptre and the crown of pride,—
Calling for the masquerade and music of his minions,—
Calling for the loves whose murdered eyes had left him
    wise
With phantasies of flesh in wind-bewailed dominions.

.   .   .   .   .

Their tongues were guttering lights; their songs were
    sated revels;
Their mimicries that sank to whispers and withdrew
Were couriers of corruption. Mocked and maimed he
    knew,
For scrawls on dungeon walls his priapismic devils.

He woke; the sceptre broke; and cast away the crown;
Fought blindly with the strangling of the scarlet gown;
Cried out on hell and heaven, and saw the burning-bright
Angel with eyes inexorable and wings, once white
For mercy, now by storming judgment backward blown;
Saw absolution changed to unrelenting stone;
Shrieked; and aghast his ghost from flesh was whirled
    away
 On roaring gales of gloom. . . . He heard an angel say . . .

THE ROAD TO RUIN

My hopes, my messengers I sent
Across the ten years continent
Of Time. In dream I saw them go,—
And thought, 'When they come back I'll know
To what far place I lead my friends
Where this disastrous decade ends'.

Like one in purgatory, I learned
The loss of hope. For none returned,
And long in darkening dream I lay.
Then came a ghost whose warning breath
Gasped from an agony of death,
'No, not that way ; no, not that way'.

1933.

'The craving for power which characterizes the governing class in every nation is hostile to any limitation of the national sovereignty. This political power-hunger is wont to batten on the activities of another group whose aspirations are on purely mercenary, economic lines. I have specially in mind that small but determined group, active in every nation, composed of individuals who, indifferent to social considerations and restraints, regard warfare, the manufacture and sale of arms, simply as an occasion to advance their personal interests and enlarge their personal authority.'

A. EINSTEIN

1. At the Cenotaph

I saw the Prince of Darkness, with his Staff,
Standing bare-headed by the Cenotaph:
Unostentatious and respectful, there
He stood, and offered up the following prayer.
 'Make them forget, O Lord, what this Memorial
  Means; their discredited ideas revive;
 Breed new belief that War is purgatorial
  Proof of the pride and power of being alive;
 Men's biologic urge to readjust
  The Map of Europe, Lord of Hosts, increase;
 Lift up their hearts in large destructive lust;
  And crown their heads with blind vindictive Peace.'
The Prince of Darkness to the Cenotaph
Bowed. As he walked away I heard him laugh.

2. Mimic Warfare

Troops on manoeuvres, mechanized and masked,
Solve tactical conundrums for the Tanks—
Plodding the Plain in patriotic pranks.

'What means this mimic warfare?' I have asked,
Halting my horse on a green ridge whose rings
Remind mankind of unenlightened Kings.

My query's abstract . . . Genial tanks go grinding
Along the tarmac. Joining in the fun,
An armoured lorry hauls an aircraft gun.
Meanwhile in summer sunlight no one's finding
Cause to disparage these unconscious provers
Of nations pledged to war's traditional crimes.
No casualties occur in such manoeuvres
(Blandly reported in to-morrow's *Times*).

3. A Premonition

A gas-proof ghost, I climbed the stair
To find how priceless paintings fare
When corpses, chemically killed,
Lie hunched and twisted in the stilled
Disaster of Trafalgar Square.

To time's eternities I came;
And found the Virgin of the Rocks
Dreaming with downward eyes the same
Apocalypse of peace . . . The claim
Of Art was disallowed. Past locks
And walls crass war had groped, and gas
Was tarnishing each gilded frame.

4. The Ultimate Atrocity

When the first man who wasn't quite an ape
Felt magnanimity and prayed for more,
The world's redemption stood, in human shape,
With darkness done and betterment before.

[202]

From then till now such men have multiplied;
From then till now their task has been the same,
In whom the world's redemption dreamed and died—
To whom the vision of perfection came.

I hear an aeroplane—what years ahead
Who knows?—but if from that machine should fall
The first bacterial bomb, this world might find
That all the aspirations of the dead
Had been betrayed and blotted out, and all
Their deeds denied who hoped for Humankind.

5. *News from the War-After-Next*

The self-appointed Representative
Of Anti-Christ in Europe having been chosen
As War Dictator, we are pledged to live
With Violence, Greed, and Ignorance as those in
Controllership of Life . . . The microphone
Transmits the creed of Anti-Christ alone.

The last Idealist was lynched this morning
By the Beelzebub's Cathedral congregation—
A most impressive and appropriate warning
To all who would debrutalize the Nation.

Our dago enemies having tried to kill us
By every method hitherto perfected,
We launch to-morrow our great new Bacillus,
And an overwhelming victory is expected.
    Thus, Moloch willing, we inaugurate
    A super-savage Mammonistic State.

6. An Unveiling

The President's oration ended thus:
'Not vainly London's War-gassed victims perished.
We are a part of them, and they of us:
As such they will perpetually be cherished.
Not many of them did much; but all did what
They could, who stood like warriors at their post
(Even when too young to walk). This hallowed spot
Commemorates a proud, though poisoned host.
   We honour here' (he paused) 'our Million Dead;
   Who, as a living poet has nobly said,
   'Are now forever London'. Our bequest
   Is to rebuild, for What-they-died-for's sake,
   A bomb-proof roofed Metropolis, and to make
   Gas-drill compulsory. *Dulce et decorum est* . . .'

7. Asking for it

Lord God whose mercy guards the virgin jungle;
Lord God whose fields with dragon's teeth are farmed;
Lord God of blockheads, bombing-planes, and bungle,
Assist us to be adequately armed.

Lord God of cruelties incomprehensible
And randomized damnations indefensible,
Perfect in us thy tyrannous technique
For torturing the innocent and weak.

God of the dear old Mastodon's morasses
Whose love pervaded pre-diluvial mud,
Grant us the power to prove, by poison gases,
The needlessness of *shedding* human blood.

8. *Litany of the Lost*

In breaking of belief in human good;
In slavedom of mankind to the machine;
In havoc of hideous tyranny withstood,
And terror of atomic doom foreseen;
Deliver us from ourselves.

Chained to the wheel of progress uncontrolled;
World masterers with a foolish frightened face;
Loud speakers, leaderless and sceptic-souled;
Aeroplane angels, crashed from glory and grace;
Deliver us from ourselves.

In blood and bone contentiousness of nations,
And commerce's competitive re-start,
Armed with our marvellous monkey innovations,
And unregenerate still in head and heart;
Deliver us from ourselves.

1945.

VIGILS

1

An Emblem

Poet, plant your tree
On the upward way;
Aromatic bay
Plant, that men may see
Beauty greenly growing
There in storm or shine,
And through boughs divine
Freedom bravely blowing.

2

Vigils

Lone heart, learning
By one light burning,
Slow discerning of worldhood's worth;
Soul, awaking
By night and taking
Roads forsaking enchanted earth:
Man, unguided
And self-divided,
Clocked by silence which tells decay;
You that keep
In a land asleep
One light burning till break of day:
You whose vigil
Is deed and sigil,

Bond and service of lives afar,—
Seek, in seeing
Your own blind being,
Peace, remote in the morning star.

3

Elected Silence

Where voices vanish into dream,
  I have discovered, from the pride
Of temporal trophydoms, this theme,
  That silence is the ultimate guide.

Allow me now much musing-space
  To shape my secrecies alone:
Allow me life apart, whose heart
  Translates instinctive tragi-tone.

How solitude can hear! O see
  How stillness unreluctant stands
Enharmonized with cloud and tree . . .
  O earth and heaven not made with hands!

4

Vigil in Spring

The night air, smelling cold with spring,
And the dark twigs of towering trees,—
When age remembers youth we bring
Aliveness back to us in these.

Leaning from windows on the gloom,
We are one with purpling woods and wet
Wild violets of our earth in whom
Aliveness wakes and wonders yet.

Inbreathed awareness, hushed and cold,
Of growth's annunciate thrust and thrill,
We lean from lifetime, growing old,
And feel your starlit magic still.

5

December Stillness

December stillness, teach me through your trees
That loom along the west, one with the land,
The veiled evangel of your mysteries.
    While nightfall, sad and spacious, on the down
    Deepens, and dusk imbues me, where I stand,
    With grave diminishings of green and brown,
    Speak, roofless Nature, your instinctive words;
    And let me learn your secret from the sky,
    Following a flock of steadfast-journeying birds
    In lone remote migration beating by.
December stillness, crossed by twilight roads,
Teach me to travel far and bear my loads.

6

It was the love of life, when I was young,
Which led me out in summer to explore
The daybreak world. A bird's first notes were sung
For childhood standing at the garden door.

That loneliness it was which made me wise
When I looked out and saw
Dark trees against the strangely brightening skies
And learnt the love of earth that is my law.

The love of life is my religion still.
Steadfast through rigorous nights, companioned only
By what I am and what I strive to be,—
I seek no mystery now beyond the hill
And wait no change but to become more lonely,
No freedom till the sleep that sets me free.

7

They were not true, those dreams, those story books of
    youth;
I left them all at home; went out to find the truth;
Slammed the green garden gate on my young years, and
    started
Along the road to search for freedom, empty-hearted.

But dreams have secret strength; they will not die so
    soon:
They haunt the quiet house through idle afternoon;
And under childhood skies their summer thoughts await
The rediscovering soul returning tired and late.

For, having grown world-wise through harshly unlearned
    illusion,
The traveller into time arrives at this conclusion,—
That life, encountered and unmasked in variant shapes,
Dissolves in dust and cloud, and thwartingly escapes.
  But in remembered eyes of youth my dreams remain.
  They were my firstling friends. I have returned again.

8

Down the glimmering staircase, past the pensive clock,
Childhood creeps on tiptoe, fumbles at the lock.
Out of night escaping, toward the arch of dawn,
What can childhood look for, over the wet lawn?

Standing in the strangeness of that garden air,
Ignorant adventure finds world wonder there:
Miles are more than distance when the cocks are crowing
And along the valley night's last goods-train going
Tells of earth untravelled and what lies beyond
Catching roach and gudgeon in the orchard pond.

9

My past has gone to bed. Upstairs in clockless rooms
My past is fast asleep. But mindsight reillumes
Here in my ruminant head the days where dust lies deep.

Sleep-walkers empty-eyed come strangely down the
      stairs.
These are my selves,—once proud, once passionate with
      young prayers,
Once vehement with vows. I know not when they died,
Those ignorant selves. . . . Meanwhile my self sits
      brooding here
In the house where I was born. Dwindling, they disappear.
Me they did not foresee. But in their looks I find
Simplicities unlearned long since and left behind.

Unwisdom

To see with different eyes
From every day,
And find in dream disguise
Worlds far away—

To walk in childhood's land
With trusting looks,
And oldly understand
Youth's fairy-books—

Thus our unwisdom brings
Release which hears
The bird that sings
In groves beyond the years.

In Sicily

Because we two can never again come back
On life's one forward track,—
Never again first-happily explore
This valley of rocks and vines and orange-trees,
Half Biblical and half Hesperides,
With dark blue seas calling from a shell-strewn shore:
By the strange power of Spring's resistless green,
Let us be true to what we have shared and seen,
And as our amulet this idyll save.
And since the unreturning day must die,
Let it for ever be lit by an evening sky,
And the wild myrtle grow upon its grave.

[214]

Farewell to Youth

After last week's long journey, spring
    Rests in the sunshine of the Square.
Out there the leaves rejoice; they bring
    Some secret spell I may not share.

I think, I'm fond of being alone
    With music and my past. And then
I see tomorrows grey like stone,
    Where virtues walk as weary men.

And while the lenten twilight falls
    On silent room and hand-propped head,
Within my heart's mysterious walls
    The dreamer that was Youth lies dead.

13

Long Ago

Birds in the world were waking;
Dawn was beyond the wood;
Youth at an open window
Tranced in the twilight stood;
Youth in springtime strangeness
Stilled in a mind-made past,
Seeing, beyond his limits,
Loveliness veiled and vast.

Youth, once mine, once wonder,
Ignorant, brimmed with tears,

Long have you wandered, laden
Head and heart with your years;
Yet in this moment's vision,
Youth at the window stands,
Unforeboding, enchanted,
Holding the world in his hands.

14

At the end of all wrong roads I came
To the gates of the garden without a name.
There, till the spell should fail, I found
Sudden Elysium, strange with sound
Of unknown birds and waters wild
With voices unresolved for rest.
There every flower was fancy's child,
And every tree was glory's guest,
And Love, by darkness undefiled,
Went like the sun from east to west.

15

War Experience

Degrees of groping thought have taught me to conclude
That when a man began in youth to learn truth crude
From life in the demented strife and ghastly glooms
Of soul-conscripting war, mechanic and volcanic,—
Not much remains, twelve winters later, of the hater
Of purgatorial pains. And somewhat softly booms
A Somme bombardment: almost unbelieved-in looms
The day-break sentry staring over Kiel Trench crater.

[216]

16

Ex-Service

Derision from the dead
Mocks armamental madness.
Redeem (each Ruler said)
Mankind. Men died to do it.
And some with glorying gladness
Bore arms for earth and bled:
But most went glumly through it
Dumbly doomed to rue it.

The darkness of their dying
Grows one with War recorded;
Whose swindled ghosts are crying
From shell-holes in the past,
Our deeds with lies were lauded,
Our bones with wrongs rewarded.
Dream voices these—denying
Dud laurels to the last.

17

Break silence. You have listened overlong
To muttering mind-wrought voices. Call for lights.
Prove these persistent haunting presences wrong
Who mock and stultify your days and nights.

Dawn comes and re-creates the sleepless room;
And eyesight asks what arguing plagues exist.
But in that garret of uneasy gloom
Which is your brain, the presences persist.

18

The Gains of Good

Word slowly understood;
Thought finding gradual form;
And power applied;
These are the gains of good;
Bold breath and life-blood **warm**;
Darkness denied.

To carve the stubborn stone;
With sense intense explore,
And inward sight.
Thus make they earth their own,
Whose deeds their dream adore,
Leaving us light.

19

'We Shall Not All Sleep'

Often I've wanted to be half a ghost,
Haunting familiar friends, unheard but hearing:
Silent among their silences. For most
I like such guesthood, freed, unfelt, unfearing.

Unfelt? Who knows? . . . If shriven self survives,
Might not a hint be given, a warning uttered
By ghostly vigilance, to troubled lives?
Might not their intuitions be half unshuttered,
And, like a dusty sunbeam on the gloom,
Death send one shaft of radiance to that room?

Unvouched are visions. But sleep-forsaken faith
Can win unworlded miracles and rejoice,
Welcoming, at haggard ends of night,—what wraith—
What angel—what beloved and banished voice?

20

Vibrations

Chord—very softly sounded—echoing on;
Touched by what hand, who knows—for what rapt ear?—
In this rayed room of memories past and gone
From thought, reanimate now and ghostly near:
Veiled musical vibrations which belong
To these essential walls, these trodden floors,
These windows open to the blackbird's song,
And, shut for the last time on life, these doors.
    Caught unaware in day-dream silences,
    I hear you, vanished voices, where such peace
    Imbues my being as when your gladness breathed;
    And now like leafy whispering it is,
    And now slow shadows of the towering trees
    On lawns that your experience has bequeathed.

21

Words for the Wordless

Smile on, you newly dead, whose griefless masks
Are emptied of mortality of mind;
Safe is your secret from the world that asks
If death be dark,—all lost and left behind.

Be dust, you ex-inhabitants of air,
You freemen of—at worst—unconscious night;
Be mystery, you whose voices haunt us where
This little while we listen from the light.

Be real, imagined angels, when we stand
Near-thoughted to the cold and cratered land,
Alone with imperfection that must part
From flesh, which for its crowned achievement cried,
And soon must follow those who dreamed and died
Carrying immortal omens in their heart.

22

Again the dead, the dead again demanding
To be, O now to be remembered strongly—
The dead, reminding mindsight of their darkness—
The dead who overhear us, listening longly.

Musician, now reverberant in our playing;
Poet, the presence haunting urgent words;
Dead youth, in love with life, now June-awakened
To hear through dream the dawn-delighted birds;
How can you be believed in, how made certain,
How sought beyond the silences of learning?
And how, revisitants by life envisioned,
Can what we are empower your quiet returning?

23
Revisitation

(W.H.R.R.)

What voice revisits me this night? What face
To my heart's room returns?
From that perpetual silence where the grace
Of human sainthood burns
Hastes he once more to harmonize and heal?
I know not. Only I feel
His influence undiminished.
And his life's work, in me and many, unfinished.

O fathering friend and scientist of good,
Who in solitude, one bygone summer's day,
And in throes of bodily anguish, passed away
From dream and conflict and research-lit lands
Of ethnologic learning,—even as you stood
Selfless and ardent, resolute and gay,
So in this hour, in strange survival stands
Your ghost, whom I am powerless to repay.

24
The Merciful Knight

Swift, in a moment's thought, our lastingness is wrought
From life, the transient wing.
Swift, in a moment's light, he mercy found, that knight
Who rode alone in spring . . .
The knight who sleeps in stone with ivy overgrown
Knew this miraculous thing.

In a moment of the years the sun, like love through tears,
Shone where the rain went by.
In a world where armoured men made swords their
    strength and then
Rode darkly out to die,
One heart was there estranged; one heart, one heart was
    changed
While the cloud crossed the sun . . .
Mercy from long ago, be mine that I may know
Life's lastingness begun.

25

Memorandum

In multitudes we grope; our blurred events
Were argued by assembled generations.
Time toils in centuries and by continents
While racial memories haunt the souls of nations.
Enormous murmurings from the mind of man
Accumulate as history; and from void
Obliquities of ignorance which began
His growth, blind hordes have laboured and destroyed.

If there should be some Power ensphered in light
Who contemplates his handiwork, supreme
In differentiating wrong from right,—
To him all human consciousness might seem
A Sleeper, powerless in imprisoning night
To waken from a purgatorial dream.

26

Human Histories

The multitudinous dead, like books unread,
Are somewhere in the library of Time.
Glimpses we get, of what they felt and said,—
Humdrum and homely, or loftily sublime:
But mostly they are ghostly, nameless, nought,
Whose journeying shadows fell and left no trace;
Whose worlds in worlds of woven and welded thought
Are now the language of a vanished race.
    Nothing exists in life more strange than these
    Lost lineaments of human histories.

27

Babylon

Babylon that was beautiful is Nothing now.
Once to the world it tolled a golden bell:
Belshazzar wore its blaze upon his brow;
Ruled; and to ruin fell.
Babylon—a blurred and blinded face of stone—
At dumb Oblivion bragged with trumpets blown;
Teemed, and while merchants throve and prophets
    dreamed,
Bowed before idols, and was overthrown.

Babylon the merciless, now a name of doom,
Built towers in Time, as we today, for whom
Auguries of self-annihilation loom.

28

The Hour-Glass

Myself I see, holding an hour-glass in his hand,
Deriving intimate omens from the trickling sand:
Intent on Time's device which casually contains
The world's enigma in its quietly falling grains.
Myself I see; for whom the idle moments pass
From *is* to *was* in that *memento mori* glass;
For whom the divination darkly seems to say,

'I am the emblem of your phantom yesterday.
I am tomorrow's journey and the eternal track
Across the desert land of life where none turn back.
I am the setting sun, the sun that rises red;
And the white moon, silvering dim cities of the dead.'

29

Everyman

The weariness of life that has no will
To climb the steepening hill:
The sickness of the soul for sleep, and to be still.
And then once more the impassioned pigmy fist
Clenched cloudward and defiant;
The pride that would prevail, the doomed protagonist
Grappling the ghostly giant.
Victim and venturer turn by turn, and then
Set free to be again
Companion in repose with those who once were men.

30

The mind of man environing its thought,
Wherein a world within this world is wrought,—
   A shadowed face alone in fields of light.
The lowly growth and long endeavour of will
That waits and watches from its human hill,
   A landmark tree looming against the night.

World undiscovered within us, radiant-white,
Through miracles of sight unmastered still,
Grant us the power to follow and to fulfil.

31

Heaven

Heaven, through the storm-rent skies of Time revealing
Visions, designed by man's death-fearing mind
To hallow his carnal heritage with healing.

Heaven, the last word upon their lips for whom
No morning-star shall burn, beyond that whisper
Going to look for angels in the gloom.

Heaven, the reward of racked renunciation,
When from the body's broken wayside shrine
The spirit in its ultimate aspiration
Shares the world-sacrifice and dies divine.

P   [225]   S.C.P.

32

Credo

The heaven for which I wait has neither guard nor gate.
The God in whom I trust shall raise me not from dust.
I shall not see that heaven for which my days have striven,
Nor kneel before the God toward whom my feet have
    trod.

But when from this half-human evolvement man and
    woman
Emerge, through brutish Me made strong and fair and
    free,
The dumb forgotten dead will be the ground they tread,
And in their eyes will shine my deathless hope divine.

33

Ultimatum

Something we cannot see, something we may not reach,
Something beyond clairvoyant vision of the years
Our senses, winged with spirit, wordlessly beseech.

Meanwhile rife rumourings of the earth are in our ears,—
The lonely beat of blood, the immanence of ghosts,
And foam's oblivion whitening under crumbling coasts.

34

Presences Perfected

I looked on that prophetic land
Where, manifested by their powers,
Presences perfected stand
Whom night and day no more command
With shine and shadow of earthly hours.

I saw them. Numberless they stood
Half-way toward heaven, that men might mark
The grandeur of their ghostlihood
Burning divinely on the dark.

Names had they none. Through spirit alone
They triumphed, the makers of mankind,
Whose robes like flames were round them blown
By winds which raved from the unknown
Erebus of earth's ancestral mind.

35

Ode

Man, frustrated and sleep-forsaken,
Gloom-regarding from inward sight,
Sees the city of God unshaken
Steeply stand in unworlded white;
Sees, adrift from his faith-lost learning,
Sun-remote from terrestrial thought,
Power, envisioned by earth's discerning,
Peace, by mortal aspiring wrought.

How dares he in a dream's deceiving
Link that vision with love unknown,—
Out of the dark in his blind believing
Claiming the city of God for his own?
How, alone with his human story,
Mazed by myths of the gods of men,
Dares he guess in that glimpse of glory
Truth revealed from beyond his ken?

Sense-confined in his brain existence,
Not for him to deny his doom;
Not through dreams does the soul outdistance
Death who knocks at the listening room.
Not from time shall he look on heaven;
Not through hope shall his faults be healed . . .
City of God, to redeemed forgiven
Radiant life, be on earth revealed.

RHYMED RUMINATIONS

Brevities

I am that man who with a luminous look
Sits up at night to write a ruminant book.

I am that man who with a furrowing frown
Thinks harshly of the world—and corks it down.

I am that man who loves to ride alone
When landscapes wear his mind's autumnal tone.

I am that man who, having lived his day,
Looks once on life and goes his wordless way.

Thoughts in 1932

Alive—and forty-five—I jogged my way
Across a dull green day,
Listening to larks and plovers, well content
With the pre-Roman pack-road where I went.

Pastoral and pleasant was the end of May.
But readers of the times had cause to say
That skies were brighter for the late Victorians;
And 'The Black Thirties' seemed a sobriquet
Likely to head the chapters of historians.

Above Stonehenge a drone of engines drew
My gaze; there seven and twenty war-planes flew
Manoeuvring in formation; and the drone
Of that neat-patterned hornet-gang was thrown
Across the golden downland like a blight.

Cities, I thought, will wait them in the night
When airmen, with high-minded motives, fight
To save Futurity. In years to come
Poor panic-stricken hordes will hear that hum,
And Fear will be synonymous with Flight.

Property

Upstairs among my books
I heard a noise of rooks
Returning to the woods.
Loud was that legion wheeling;
And queer my inward feeling—
'These windows are revealing
My chattels and my goods.'

Possession thus we claim
Of natural sights and sounds,
Who purchase earth with pounds
And take it all for granted.
We nothings use a name,
Nor ask whence acorns came
Before the oak was planted.

Outlived by Trees

A beech, a cedar, and a lime
Grow on my lawn, embodying time.
A lime, a cedar, and a beech
The transience of this lifetime teach.

Beech, cedar, lime, when I'm dead Me,
You'll stand, lawn-shadowing, tree by tree;
And in your greenery, while you last,
I shall survive who shared your past.

Eulogy of My House

House, though you've harboured grave-yards-full of lives
Since on your first foundations walls were built,
In your essential atmosphere survives
No sense of men's malignity and guilt.
Bad times you must have known, and human wrongness;
Yet your plain wisdom leaves it all behind you,
Within whose walls tranquillity and strongness
Keep watch on life. Dependable I find you.

Much good has been your making. I can feel
That when your ghosts revisit you they steal
From room to room like moonlight long ago:
And if some voice from silence haunts my head
I only wonder who it was that said—
'House, I am here because I loved you so.'

[233]

In Heytesbury Wood

Not less nor more than five and forty years ago
The old lord went along the ornamental ride;
For the last time he walked there, tired and very slow;
Saw the laburnum's golden chains, the glooming green
Of bowery box-trees; stood and looked farewell, and
    sighed
For roots that held his heart and summers that he'd seen.

And then, maybe, he came again there, year by year,
To watch, as dead men do, and see—who knows how
    clear?—
That vista'd paradise which in his time had thriven;
Those trees to which in cogitating strolls he'd given
Perennial forethought,—branches that he'd lopped and
    cherished:
Came, and saw sad neglect; dense nettles; favourites
    felled
Or fallen in gales and left to rot; came and beheld
How with succeeding seasons his laburnums perished.

'Return', I think, 'next summer, and you'll find such
    change,—
Walking, some low-lit evening, in the whispering
    wood,—
As will refresh your eyes and do them ghostly good;
See redolence befriend, neglect no more estrange;
See plumed acacia and the nobly tranquil bay;
Laburnums too, now small as in the prosperous prime
Of your well-ordered distant mid-Victorian time . . .'

Thus I evoke him; thus he looks and goes his way
Along that path we call the ornamental ride—
The old slow lord, the ghost whose trees were once
   his pride.

While Reading a Ghost Story

Opening my window for a breath of air
I meet the midnight cold, and am aware
Of wind-shook trees and harmless lonely stars.
There's nothing monstrous moving; nothing mars
This friendly blustering of mid-winter gloom.
   Behind me, in the comfort of my room,
    A story I've been reading lies half read . . .
   Corrupt revisitation by the dead.

Old houses have their secrets. Passions haunt them.
When day's celestials go, abhorred ones taunt them.
Inside our habitations darkness dwells.
While dusk of dawn is on the unwatched stair
And lofty windows whiten strangely,—there
What presence thins—with what frustrated spells?

On Edington Hill

   Stars wink beyond the downland barrows
   Where Alfred marched to meet the Danes,
   Far in advance of flinthead arrows
   And unaware of aeroplanes.

[235]

Now the white owl on silent wing
Crosses the looming lonely track;
And here our anti-pagan king
Beat the red-handed plunderers back.

That Eastertide—historians write—
He saved the future by the sword
Which emblemed in barbaric night
The cross of Jesus Christ his Lord.
That was the crucial point, men say:
For Alfred's wisdom was his crown,
Who, in the old skull-shattering way,
Christened the powers of darkness down.

Dawn breaks where tribes once fought with flints;
Where Alfred smote, the white owl flits
Whose instincts are as old as time.
And we—to-day's historian hints—
May all be Alfreds, bombed to bits
In conflict with a creed of crime.

1935.

878-1935

Here, on his march to Eathundun, King Alfred passed:
No wood was planted then; the terraced hill was grassed.
Now, in the summer, tanks come lumbering down the
    lane.
I'd like to watch King Alfred walk this way again.

Then, it was quite correct to hack and hew the Dane,
And to be levied for a war was life's event.
Now in a world of books I try to live content,
And hear uneasily the droning aeroplane.

I'd rather die than be some dim ninth-century thane;
Nor do I envy those who fought at Eathundun.
Yet I have wondered, when was Wiltshire more insane
Than now—when world ideas like wolves are on the run?

Silver Jubilee Celebration

(AT THE DINNER OF THE ROYAL SOCIETY OF ST. GEORGE)

Broadcast across the as yet unbeaconed dark,
I heard the shout of that symposiarch
Whose voice, like some Gargantuan-mouthed grotesque,
Demanded silence for the honoured guest.
Then—when prolonged applauding had subsided—
Kipling, that legendary name, confided
In us—a host of atmospheric ears—
His planned post-mortem on the post-war years.

Suavely severe—not one bleak syllable blurred—
In dulcet-bitter and prophetic tones
(Each word full charged with dynamite deferred)
He disinterred a battlefield of bones . . .
And then reminded us that our attempt
To put all war behind us with the last one
Had been a dream administrators dreamt;
In fact a virtuous fallacy—and a vast one.

[237]

Meanwhile his audience, mystified at first,
Sat spell-bound while he preached with barbed
      conviction,
Who, through implied anathemas, re-cursed
Our old opponents in that four years' friction.
And if indeed it was the astringent truth
He told with such incomparable concision—
That we must now re-educate our youth
With 'Arm or perish' as their ultimate vision—
Let us at least be candid with the world
And stitch across each Union Jack unfurled
'No bargain struck with Potsdam is put over
Unless well backed by bombers—and Jehovah!'

A Remembered Queen

If I could see that wild and warring Queen
Who lived here for a time, old histories claim;
If she, revisioned by my thought, could come!

Did voices walk the air, released from death,
Hers might be heard when, very late at night,
I turn the wireless on and catch no sound
But atmospheric cracklings, moans, and thuds.
Hers might be heard, associate with this ground
Whereon her house once stood. Eight hundred year
Are not so far, in terms of light from star.

Like moonlight on the low mist in the park
Is that remembered fierce twelfth-century Queen
Who lived here once, men say. If on the dark

I heard shrill Norman French and stood between
That utterance and eternity! If, so
Attuned, I could watch Queen Matilda go
Hunched on her horse across the crunching snow!

Prehistoric Burials

These barrows of the century-darkened dead,—
Memorials of oblivion, these turfed tombs
Of muttering ancestries whose fires, once red,
Now burn for me beyond mysterious glooms;
   I pass them day by day while daylight fills
   My sense of sight on these time-haunted hills.

Could I but watch those burials that began
Whole history—flint and bronze and iron beginnings,
When under this wide Wiltshire sky crude man
Warred with his world and augured our world-winnings!
Could I but enter that unholpen brain,
Cabined and comfortless and insecure,
That ruled some settlement on Salisbury Plain
And offered blood to blind primeval powers,—
Dim Caliban whose doom was to endure
Earth's ignorant nullity made strange with flowers.

Antiquities

Enormous aqueducts have had their day,
And moles make mounds where marshals camped and
   clashed.

On stones where awe-struck emperors knelt to pray
The tourist gapes with guide-book, unabashed.
Historian Time, who in his 'Life of Man'
Records the whole, himself is much unread:
The breath must go from beauty, and the span
Of Lethe bleaken over all the dead.

Only the shattered arch remains to tell
Humanity its transience and to be
Life-work for archaeologists who spell
The carven hieroglyphics of Chaldee.
And where the toiling town once seethed in smoke
There'll drop, through quiet, one acorn from an oak.

A Local Train of Thought

Alone, in silence, at a certain time of night,
Listening, and looking up from what I'm trying to write,
I hear a local train along the Valley. And 'There
Goes the one-fifty', think I to myself; aware
That somehow its habitual travelling comforts me,
Making my world seem safer, homelier, sure to be
The same to-morrow; and the same, one hopes, next
    year.
'There's peacetime in that train.' One hears it disappear
With needless warning whistle and rail-resounding
    wheels.
'That train's quite like an old familiar friend', one feels.

Thoughts in 1938

A man's mood can be not unlike the place, the time of
    day, the weather:
One afternoon, toward sundown, these were toned for
    me, all three together.
Riding with ruminant mind, I stared at Salisbury Plain's
    November distance,
By solitude imbued, responsive to my world without
    resistance.

Mild weather after wind and rain; earth, sky, and season
    all quiescent.
'If this be my biography.' I mused, 'to pace along is
    pleasant;
And after all, my unambitious mid-maturity deserves
—If luck befriends me thus—this liberal landscape's
    contour lines and curves.'

There on that ancient drove-road, leading to nowhere
    now, my horse
Grazed and then gazed, as I did, over the quietly coloured
    miles.
Though sign-posts pointed toward the dread of war,
    ourselves, of course,
Were only humdrum joggers on through time.
    Remembering it one smiles.

'A View of Old Exeter'

Pyne, a small honest painter, well content
To limn our English landscapes, worked and went,
From 1800 onward, seventy years,
Then left the world to louden in men's ears.
Here's his 'Old Exeter'; much eyed by me
Since (how time flits!) full fifteen years ago
I bought it cheap and carried it home to be
A window on my wall making me know
Old Exeter, affectionately recorded
In the now slow paced 'fifties.
                        Glancing down
From some neglected meadow near the town,
He hummed and sketched that I might be afforded
This purview of the past's provincial peace.

For J. B. Pyne Old Exeter was good;
Cows in his foreground grazed and strolled and stood:
For J. B. Pyne Victorian clumps of trees
Were golden in a bland October breeze:
Large clouds, like safe investments, loitered by;
And distant Dartmoor loomed in sombre blue.
Perpetuator of that shifting sky,
It never crossed his mind that he might do
From death such things as make me stare and sigh,—
Sigh for that afternoon he thus depicted,—
That simpler world from which we've been evicted.

Here his prim figures cruise and sit and drive
In crinolines as when they were alive.

Out of the town that man and wife are going
In smart new gig, complacently unknowing
Of their great-grandchild's air-raid-worried mind:
Into the town those gentlewomen are walking
Attuned to life, of the new Bishop talking—
Pleased that the eighteenth century's left behind,
And civically unconscious, I conjecture,
Of what it gave them in good architecture.
That group beside the cypresses adds calm
And absent-minded momentary charm
To the industrious artist's composition . . .
When J. B. Pyne's, this was a Devon Day.
For me it shines far far—too far—away;
For time has changed this 'View' into a Vision.

Metamorphosis

Sandys sat translating Ovid. Both his hands
Were busy. Busy was his curious mind.
Each note he wrote was news from fabled lands.
He hob-nobbed with Pythagoras, calm and kind.
In a quaint narrow age, remote from this,
Sat Sandys translating *Metamorphosis*.

The scholarship is obsolete, and the verse
Pedestrian perhaps. Yet, while I turn
His friendly folio pages (none the worse
For emblematic worm-holes) I discern
Not Nature preying on itself, but Time
Revealed by rich humanity in rhyme.

Ideologies

'I've an idea!' cried someone long ago
In liveliest monkey-language. What he thought
Caused chatter. What it was we do not know.
But this was the earliest ape on earth who brought
Experimental notions into play.
Nature ignored him, as she does to-day.

When Man's at last learnt how to make his mind,
Nature may listen to thought and serve its needs.
Meanwhile where Babels once were built we find
A spider in his web among the weeds.

Two Old Ladies

Here's an old lady, almost ninety-one.
Fragile in dark blue velvet, from her chair
She talks to me about Lord Palmerston,
With whom her father 'often took the air'.
I watch her tiny black-lace-mittened hands—
When tea-time's ended—slowly crumble a rusk
For feeding peacocks with. Reflective stands
My memory-mirror in the autumn dusk.

Memory records the scene; and straightway plays
One of its dream-like unexpected tricks;
Transports me forty years to summer days
On time's first page, when I was only six . . .

Miss Clara, deaf and old, alert and queer,
With scraps of bread heaped on a dark blue dish,
Conducts me—I can catch her voice quite clear—
Out to the lily-pond to feed the fish.

Blunden's Beech

I named it Blunden's Beech; and no one knew
That this—of local beeches—was the best.
Remembering lines by Clare, I'd sometimes rest
Contentful on the cushioned moss that grew
Between its roots. Finches, a flitting crew,
Chirped their concerns. Wiltshire, from east to west
Contained my tree. And Edmund never guessed
How he was there with me till dusk and dew.

Thus, fancy-free from ownership and claim,
The mind can make its legends live and sing
And grow to be the genius of some place.
And thus, where sylvan shadows held a name,
The thought of Poetry will dwell, and bring
To summer's idyll an unheeded grace.

November Dusk

Ruminant, while firelight glows on shadowy walls
And dusk with the last leaves of autumn falls,
I hear my garden thrush whose notes again
Tell stillness after hours of gusty rain.

[245]

Can I record tranquillity intense
With harmony of heart,—experience
Like a rich memory's mind-lit monochrome?
Winged lovely moments, can I call you home?

This texture is to-day's. Near as my mind
Each instant is; yet each reveals to me
November night-falls known a lifetime long:
And I've no need to travel far to find
This bird who from the leafless walnut tree
Sings like the world's farewell to sight and song.

Wealth of Awareness

Stars burning bright in summer night; and I
Standing alone with lifetime on this lawn;
Smelling the dew that soaks the sunburnt grass,
Alone with moth-winged gloom and folded flowers
And secret stirrings, hours away from dawn.

One with these garden silences that pass,
I know that life is in my saturate sense
Of growth and memories of what lifetime meant.
I am yet young with my unheard unspent
Awareness of slow-stored intransience:
And still, where trees like sentinels look for day,
I feel what all have felt and know what none can say.

Acceptance

Can happiness be mine when the restless body tires,
And, wearied of the wine of dangerous desires,
I turn toward heights that shine with unbefriending fires?

I have looked and understood how happiness recedes;
Not like the shore we leave at sunset; not by deeds
Of anger or indifference darkened into death,
But taken away by time,—O given back like breath.

Heart and Soul

Growing older, the heart's not colder:
Losing youngness, the eye sees clearer.
   (Inward eye, while our sight grows blurred.)
Living longer, the soul grows stronger.
Looked on, the darkening weald grows dearer.
   (Weald of youth, a remembered word.)

Soul undaunted and heart death-haunted
Dwell together, estranged yet one.
   (Starlight lonely and firelit room.)
Heart, be brave as you go to your grave;
Soul, be girt for the race unrun.
   (Holpen both by ghosts from the gloom.)

A Picture of the Muses

In an empty room upstairs,
While the sunshine dozes lonely
And on summer evening airs
Time is heard in rumours only,
Still unframed, my mother's 'Muses'
In their world of dawn and roses
Reinvoke an old idyllic
Rapture that my life now loses.

Long ago the flush of day-break
Bloomed beyond those calm shapes pacing.
Now, in empty room and evening,
I, that grievening vision facing,
Stand in memory's moment halted,
By my dreams no more exalted.

Tragitones

I have not sought these quietened cadences,
These tragitones, these stilled interior themes,
These vistas where imagined presences
Lead me away from life,—loved ghosts or dreams?

Look where the light of June is in the leaves,
And how the world with laughter hurries on.
The grass is golden; yet my faith perceives
No foot-print where felicity has gone.

Midsummer Eve

Time, you timeless old mower of all that we men love
    most,
Are you indeed the Unknower, or a wisely garnering
    ghost?

On Midsummer Eve you are symbol of centuries carried
    like hay:
And all the year round you are nimble, fetching our
    spirits away
To the unknown land of death where you are a locked-out
    stranger . . .
O Time, you bringer of breath, you ever-unchanging
    changer!

Old World to New

Two thousand years ahead, maybe,
Some man looks back toward myriad Me,
And thinks, 'I'd give a lot to know
What life was like—that time ago!'

Beyond our monuments destroyed,
Beyond Utopia gained and lost,
And cheerful centuries well employed
In paying what men's folly cost,—
O face no more humane than this,
O heart no less deceived than mine,

[249]

O spirit brinked by death's abyss,
O eyes which earth and cloud confine,—
From your world order gazing back,
Learn, and forgive me what I lack.

A Prayer from 1936

We are souls in hell; who hear no gradual music
Advancing on the air, on wave-lengths walking.
We are lost in life; who listen for hope and hear but
The tyrant and the politician talking.

Out of the nothingness of night they tell
Our need of guns, our servitude to strife.
O heaven of music, absolve us from this hell
Unto unmechanized mastery over life.

Earth and Heaven

What harmonies of earth are heard in heaven? . . .
If heaven there be, it is not strange nor far;
Much nearer is it than the morning star,
And human as our hearts which die forgiven.

O if there be that other world, that grace
Of souls redeemed, we breathe it like the air;
And angels are about us everywhere
In love's good deeds, in life's transfigured face.

[250]

Gloria Mundi

Who needs words in autumn woods
When colour concludes decay?
There old stories are told in glories
For winds to scatter away.

Wisdom narrows where downland barrows
Image the world's endeavour.
There time's tales are as light that fails
On faces fading forever.

Meeting and Parting

My self reborn, I look into your eyes;
While you, unknowing, look your first time on me.
Thus will *you* stand when life within me dies,
And you, full knowing, my parting presence see.

Alone I stand before my new-born son;
Alone he lies before me, doomed to live.
Beloved, when I am dying and all is done,
Look on my face and say that you forgive.

To My Son

Go, and be gay;
You are born into the dazzling light of day.

Go, and be wise;
You are born upon an earth which needs new eyes.
Go, and be strong;
You are born into a world where love rights wrong.
Go, and be brave;
Possess your soul; that you alone can save.

A Blessing

Your little flame of life we guard
For the long night that must be hard:
Your eyes we teach to know the day
That shall make wonderful your way.
Bright be your flame, my soul, my son,
Whose pilgrimage I see begun:
And when these guiding hands are gone,
In love of all things good go on.

The Child at the Window

Remember this, when childhood's far away;
The sunlight of a showery first spring day;
You from your house-top window laughing down,
And I, returned with whip-cracks from a ride,
On the great lawn below you, playing the clown.
Time blots our gladness out. Let this with love abide . . .

The brave March day; and you, not four years old,
Up in your nursery world—all heaven for me.
Remember this—the happiness I hold—
In far off springs I shall not live to see;
The world one map of wastening war unrolled,
And you, unconscious of it, setting my spirit free.

For you must learn, beyond bewildering years,
How little things beloved and held are best.
The windows of the world are blurred with tears,
And troubles come like cloud-banks from the west.
Remember this, some afternoon in spring,
When your own child looks down and makes your sad
     heart sing.

Progressions

A lovely child alone, singing to himself serenely,—
Playing with pebbles in an unfrequented garden
Through drowse of summer afternoon where time drifts
     greenly.

A youth, impassioned by he knows not what, exploring
Delusive labyrinths in errors age will pardon,—
A youth, all ignorance, all grace, his dreams adoring.

A man, confounded by the facts of life that bind him
Prometheus-like to rocks where vulture doubts assail
     him,—
A man, with blank discarded youthfulness behind him.

A mind, matured in wearying bones, returning slowly
Toward years revisioned richly while fruitions fail him,—
A mind, renouncing hopes and finding lost loves holy.

Silly Sooth

Do not deny your dreams
That are the absurd release
From worldly wisdom themes
To paradoxic peace.

When sleep invites your mind
To push the unhaspèd door,
Be glad to leave behind
The unrest of Evermore.

There in that reasonless clime
You are yourself; and thither
You float, set free from Time
And all its whence and whither.

Farewell to hands and feet;
Good-bye to mouth and eyes.
Dreamer, go forth to greet
What world within you lies.

Old Music

Like the notes of an old violin,
Thoughts talk to me within
My mind, that shuttered room.
Like luminous portraits, hung
On walls where I once was young,
Dead friends pervade the gloom.

Decades of mellowing went
To make this calmed content,
This mental vintagement
Of youth's harsh tasting wine . . .
Old violin, play on
Till heart-held thought be gone:
Old friends whose charity shone
For me, be memory-mine.

Doggerel About Old Days

Young people now—they don't know what the past was
    like.
Then one could find the main roads museful on one's bike.
Give me a moment and I'm back in Kent; I know
How safe and sound life struck me thirty years ago.

Passenger trains puffed on through landscapes then like
    Time;
And this year with its next year found an easy rhyme.

[255]

Uninterrupted cricket seasons were to come.
Beanfields were good to smell and bees would always hum
In trees that knew no threat of overhead invasion.
One liked the foreground future, needing no persuasion.

Kent was all sleepy villages through which I went
Carrying my cricket-bag. In wintertime, content
To follow hounds across wet fields, I jogged home tired.
In 1909 the future was a thing desired.

I travelled on; the train was Time; Kent was the scene;
And where I was I felt that, as I'd always been,
I should continue unperturbed in storm and shine.
Will someone tell me where I am—in '39?

The English Spirit

Apollyon having decided to employ
His anger of blind armaments for this—
That every valued virtue and guarded joy
Might grieve bewildered by a bombed abyss—
    The ghosts of those who have wrought our English Past
    Stand near us now in unimpassioned ranks
    Till we have braved and broken and overcast
    The cultural crusade of Teuton tanks.

May 19, 1940.

Silent Service

Now, multifold, let Britain's patient power
Be proven within us for the world to see.
None are exempt from service in this hour;
And vanquished in ourselves we dare not be.
  Now, for a sunlit future, we can show
  The clenched resolved endurance that defies
Daemons in dark,—and toward that future go
With earth's defended freedom in our eyes.
  In every separate soul let courage shine—
  A kneeling angel holding faith's front-line.

May 23, 1940.

Eyes

Narcissus youth has looked at life and seen
In the strange mirror only his own stare,—
His own unanswering gaze whose circled green
Contains two tiny pictures of the scene
Where youth sits dumb, only of himself aware.

Prophetic age will bid the glass good-bye
And read his microscopic tales of being
In every face but that which answers 'I',
Earning achievement from the art of seeing.
In every face he fathoms, age will throne
The intensely sphered reflection of his own
Life-labour toward unsealed intelligence.
For life sits faithful in old eyes, alone
With mortal frailty and magnificence.

Index of First Lines

Entering the strawberry-foliate demesne, 146
Evening was in the wood, louring with storm, 47
Everyone suddenly burst out singing; 124

Faces irresolute and unperplexed, 149
'Fall in! Now get a move on.' (Curse the rain.), 102
'Fall in, that awkward squad, and strike no more, 30
Fires in the dark you build; tall quivering flames, 106
For Morn, my dome of blue, 56
Frail Travellers, deftly flickering over the flowers; 111
From you, Beethoven, Bach, Mozart, 92

Give me your hand, my brother, search my face; 11
Go, and be gay; 251
God with a Roll of Honour in His hand, 80
'Good-morning; good-morning!' the General said, 75
Groping along the tunnel, step by step, 69
Growing older, the heart's not colder:, 247

Hark, hark, the Mark in the Money Market sings! 166
Have you forgotten yet? . . ., 118
He drowsed and was aware of silence heaped, 34
He heard an angel say now look for love, and look, 196
He primmed his loose red mouth and leaned his head, 27
He seemed so certain 'all was going well', 77
He staggered in from night and frost and fog, 24
He stood alone in some queer sunless place, 26
He turned to me with his kind, sleepy gaze, 17
He woke; the clank and racket of the train, 29
Heaven, through the storm-rent skies of Time revealing,
    225
'He'd never seen so many dead before.', 73

[263]

[265]

[267]

[268]